Embracing This Special Life

Learning to Flourish as a Mother of a Child with Special Needs

Jenn Soehnlin

Embracing This Special Life: Learning to Flourish as a Mother of a Child with Special Needs

Cover and Interior Design by Timothy Soehnlin

Edited by Sandra Peoples

This book is dedicated with love to my boys. Words could never express how proud and blessed I am to be your mom. I love you always and forever.

Table of Contents

Chapter 1

Why Embrace and Release?

When I learned I was going to be a mommy, the excitement was indescribable. I imagined the play dates and fun craft projects and adventures and the lessons I would teach my children. The moment that precious bundle of joy was placed in my arms, I was in love and had found a new purpose in my life.

I loved my son with all my heart and I loved being a mother, but it didn't take long before we noticed he was behind on meeting some motor milestones. He started physical therapy at nine months and speech therapy a few months later. He was diagnosed with hypotonia, a speech delay, and hearing loss.

He was two years old, hadn't said a single word, and had just started walking when my second precious baby boy was placed in my arms. I loved my new son fiercely, but I was overwhelmed with juggling a newborn and a toddler with special needs, in a new state where we had yet to find a new home church or friends.

It was a very challenging time for me and my husband, and we argued frequently that first year after we moved.

As if our life wasn't crazy enough, my older son would receive a diagnosis of apraxia of speech (a neurological speech disorder that would require years of frequent, specific and intensive speech therapy to learn how to speak), sensory processing disorder, and a few other diagnoses sprinkled in for good measure.

And, not to be left out by his big brother, my younger son would get a few diagnoses of his own: first a speech delay and sensory processing disorder, and then eventually autism.

My daydreams of motherhood were shattered, replaced with endless therapy appointments for both boys, battles with our insurance company, and an overwhelming loneliness I didn't know how to handle as a social extrovert. I had two young children with a dozen diagnoses between the two of them. My marriage was struggling. My emotional, spiritual, and physical health were rapidly declining with all the stress. Anxiety and depression took turns settling in and made themselves cozy.

I was desperate for God and yet bitter at the life He had given me, His silence, and His distance. I found myself asking Him over and over "Why?" and "Where are you?" He didn't answer and I began to have a crisis of faith. My faith wavered between trusting in God, to wondering if God really was a good God, and most terrifying of all, wondering if God even existed and my entire Christian life had been a lie. I didn't want to give up on God, but I felt He had given up on me.

Embrace

One early summer day my husband suggested we take the boys on a vacation to the beach. Inside I cringed. It sounded terrible. I envisioned chasing two little boys, ages two and four, both with speech and gross motor delays and sensory processing issues, around a beach. Oh yeah, and they both freak out if they get water in their faces. Did my dear husband realize there'd be a lot of water to get in little faces at the beach and the pool?

I thought he was crazy, and I told him so. But I also told him he worked hard for our family, and if this is what he wanted to do with his hard-earned money, then I'd honor his desire for a family vacation.

But, praise the Lord, it was a glorious vacation! The boys had a blast. Never had we seen such excitement on those little faces. "Where are we going?" my husband would ask the boys as we put on swimsuits and gathered our towels and sand toys. "Da beee!" my four-year-old son would exclaim, wiggling and doing his awkward yet charming interpretation of swimming strokes. This child, who used to be terrified of water, was soon courageously jumping into the pool into his daddy's arms. And my younger son added three words to his sparse vocabulary and learned to accept water splashed into his face without a meltdown, huge victories in our book. Huge.

My husband and I marveled at the excitement. We hadn't experienced such joy in a long time. We knew this was a gift from

God. An opportunity to enjoy our family, the progress our children were making with all the hard work and the never-ending therapies we were doing. A time to just rest and be a family.

On the last day of our trip, the thought of packing up our belongings and heading back to our house, the appointments, and the mountain of laundry gave me a panic attack. Literally.

My chest felt tight and my heart pounded. Tears streamed down my face and I couldn't catch my breath. My husband suggested I go out to the beach and spend some time by myself. I went gladly, eager to process this overwhelming anxiety with God.

I listened to the waves crash on the shore, tasted my warm salty tears. I didn't even know what to pray about. I expected more silence from God.

Never have I been more thankful to be proven wrong. He whispered one word that broke the silence and banished the anxiety and grief that had gripped my heart for so long.

Embrace.

Embrace what? I wondered.

And for the next hour or so, God revealed area after area of my life that I needed to embrace. I wish I had written in at all down at the time, but I don't think my pen would have flown across the pages fast enough. I was convicted. Encouraged. Loved by the God of the universe.

He would gently remind me of something I needed to embrace

fully in my life. Something that I needed to not only accept, but cherish. My role as a mother. My husband and his personality. My children. Their progress. Their personalities. This special-needs journey. Myself. And most importantly, God. My perspective was transformed to the biblical, rather than the worldly way of doing things that I'd been trying to do unsuccessfully for years.

I don't know how long I spent on the beach, tears rolling down my cheeks, anxious thoughts stilling, transformation unfolding in my heart. A couple hours at least. I probably could have spent longer, but it started to rain and I headed back toward our lovely beach condo where my family and a renewed purpose were waiting for me.

For the first time in a long time I felt alive and happy and at peace.

I began to live with the intention of embracing this special life I had been given.

Release

Within a few months of this beach encounter with God, as I kept striving to embrace all that God had for me, I felt like something was missing. And I found my answer in Lysa TerKeurst's best-selling book *The Best Yes*. She says:

A few years ago I traveled to visit a friend in Connecticut. As soon as she picked me up from the airport and we started driving, I saw the fallout from the storm she'd tried to describe–a massive twenty-inch snow in the middle of fall. But it wasn't the amount of snow still on the ground, or the snowmen still proudly standing, or the huge snowbanks on either side of the road that grabbed my attention.

It was the broken trees. The branches were piled everywhere. House after house. All down the street. Disastrous piles of limbs–big piles of trees–all still clinging to the leaves that hadn't dropped yet. And because the leaves hadn't dropped, the trees broke.

That's what happens when a snow comes early. The trees weren't designed to face snow before releasing their leaves. They weren't made to carry more than they should. And neither are we.

I know the weight of carrying more than I should. And usually it's because I've refused to release something before taking on something else. [1]

Oh, how I've felt broken and cracked at my core on this special needs journey. Yet another diagnosis adds to the weight. Every time I compare my child to a neurotypical child, the jealousy and the bitterness adds to the weight. Another argument with my husband over therapies and finances and the management of our home adds to the weight. Every time I feel like I'm not doing enough for my children it adds to the crushing weight. Every time I see how far we still have to go to catch up to peers, it adds to the weight. Every evaluation that reveals our childrens' strengths, but also their many weaknesses, adds to the weight.

Every time I slip into a pit of depression or paralyzing anxiety, I'm left feeling like those broken trees.

Lysa's words reminded me that you can't open your arms to something, can't truly embrace all life has to offer and flourish, until your arms aren't holding on to a bunch of things you don't need. That's when I learned the value of releasing things that did not benefit me or my family. I couldn't really embrace my children until I released my expectations and dreams I'd had for them. I couldn't embrace myself as a mother and a wife and a daughter of God until I could release my guilt and insecurities. I couldn't embrace peace and joy and thankfulness until I could release the anxiety and grief and bitterness that had overtaken my heart. I couldn't embrace God until I had released my anger and bitterness.

I have no problem admitting I haven't mastered this practice of embracing and releasing. I still struggle. I'm nowhere near where I want to be on this journey. But I'm learning to slowly let go of the stuff that God doesn't want me to hold on to. To release the junk in my life, so I can embrace His best for me. So I can embrace God's love, His plan for my children, His purpose for me, and so much more. So I can embrace God again.

Embrace and Release

The themes of embrace and release are the foundation for this book. Each chapter will alternate between something we are to release and then something we are to embrace to live a life of victory and joy and be able to flourish in this one life we've been given.

I know we each had different reactions to the realization that life would not be easy for our children. Our children may have one diagnosis, several, or have no diagnosis yet. The diagnoses may be lifelong, or able to be overcome with lots of hard work, or may be terminal. We may have one child or several with special needs. It's not so much about comparing our children's journeys with one another as it is about looking into our own heart about how we are handling this journey, and if we are processing our emotions and thoughts in a godly or worldly way.

In Ecclesiastes chapter 3, God gives us permission to experience both sides of a situation. He says:

> There is a time for everything,
> and a season for every activity under heaven:
> a time to be born and a time to die,
> a time to plant and a time to uproot,
> a time to kill and a time to heal,
> a time to tear down and a time to build,
> a time to weep and a time to laugh,
> a time to mourn and a time to dance,
> a time to scatter stones and a time to gather them,
> a time to embrace and a time to refrain,
> time to search and a time to give up [release],
> a time to keep and a time to throw away [release],
> a time to tear and a time to mend,

a time to be silent and a time to speak,

a time to love and a time to hate,

a time for war and a time for peace (Ecclesiastes 3:1-8, emphasis mine).

God Himself gives us permission to mourn and to dance. To weep and to laugh. To embrace and to refrain from embracing. To keep and to release. So don't feel bad if you're not ready to release something yet or to embrace something yet. As long as you're seeking God, it's all good. And that's what we're doing in this book. But if you can't embrace or release something yet, mark that chapter so you remember to come back to it later when you are ready. This is about your journey. Your growth. Don't feel bad if you're not ready. God says there's a time for everything. Embrace that.

Each chapter will also end with some reflection questions. You may answer them alone or find a special needs mama friend or group to discuss the answers together. These questions are to help you make the stories and truths of this book applicable to your own life. I encourage you to take your time as you answer the questions. Reflect. Pray. And embrace or release whatever God is bringing to your heart and mind.

Reflection Questions

1. What has your own journey been like?
2. What things are you wanting or needing to release?

3. What things do you want or need to embrace?

4. Based on the passage in *Ecclesiastes 3*, what season(s) do you feel you are in?

Chapter 2

Releasing Unhealthy Emotions

When I had appendicitis, I found pushing on the area the pain radiated from helped. Anytime I let go of the spot, the pain doubled in its intensity. So I lay curled in the fetal position, pressing onto the aching spot, barely able to focus on anything else, while doctors and nurses ran painful tests to figure out what exactly was going on. I thought they were crazy when they asked me to lay flat so they could do an ultrasound. It felt so unnatural to lay flat and exposed, while they pushed and prodded on the painful spot. I just wanted to be left alone, curled into a tight ball and have the pain magically disappear.

Emotional pain is similar. It can be paralyzing, preventing you from taking action and moving forward. It causes you to focus inward, on your negative emotions rather than on what is logical.

Or, the opposite reaction to pain can occur and we lash out in anger and frustration at the people around us. The expression "hurt people hurt people" is very real.

We live in a world where there is pain–both physical and emotional. We are not promised an easy life. In fact the Bible makes it clear that there will be pain and sorrow in our lives. When your child receives a diagnosis or any unfortunate circumstance shows up in our lives, emotional pain will follow. It's how we respond to that pain that matters.

David had a lot of painful experiences in his life. He had been appointed to be the next king as a child, had triumphantly defeated Goliath the giant in faith, and yet he wouldn't take the throne until he was thirty. He spent about twenty years running away from King Saul (his own father-in-law), hiding in a desert. Talk about feeling betrayed, alone, and wondering why God would choose him to be king and then bring all this upon him.

We find David amid another painful experience during his time in the desert in *1 Samuel 30*, one that gives us a picture of four types of negative emotions a person can experience when something unfortunate and unexpected happens and the effect it can have on us.

Releasing Unhealthy Grief

David and his small, loyal army would travel from time to time to fight in various battles. This time, they had been making an alliance with the Philistine leader, Achich, before returning back to their own land and family in Ziklag.

When David and his men arrived home at their town of Ziklag, they found that the Amalekites had made a raid into the Negev and Ziklag; they had crushed Ziklag and burned it to the ground. They had carried off the women and children and everyone else, without killing anyone. When David and his men saw the ruins and realized what had happened to their families, they wept until they could weep no more. David's two wives, Ahinoam from Jezreel and Abigail, the widow of Nabel from Carmel, were among those captured ... (1 Samuel 30:3-6).

The immediate response for all these men was grief. They all wept. They were all devastated that their beloved family members were captured.

Grief is defined as a deep sorrow. Synonyms include heartbreak, sadness, despair. It is a natural and healthy emotion to experience when you have experienced loss. This could include the loss of a family member or the loss of what you imagined life as a mother would be like. I remember when we received one of my oldest son's diagnoses, as soon as I was alone I wept. Life would never be the same for us, and all my dreams I had for my son needed to change. I took an opportunity to grieve before I could step into what I call my "mama bear advocating for my cub" mode.

I love the last line of *1 Samuel 30:6*, "But David found strength in the Lord." After David wept, he strengthened himself in the Lord. I like to think he wrote a psalm as one of his ways of strengthening himself.

Psalm after Psalm is filled with David admitting his emotions, but always confessing his trust in God. Always ending with praise on his lips. I want to grieve like David.

In John chapter 11, Mary and Martha have a servant inform Jesus that their brother Lazarus is dying. They expected Jesus to come running and heal their brother. He didn't and Lazarus died and was buried for four days before Jesus showed up on the scene.

When Jesus sees Mary and Martha's tears, their grief, He doesn't shame them for it. He knows these women love Him and trust Him, and He loves them too, and so He enters into their grief. In verse 35 He weeps along with them. He shares in their sorrow. The King of the universe cried with them. And then He did what only the King of the universe could do. He raised Lazarus from the dead. What victory!!

Grieving is natural and healthy. Jesus grieved. God is grieved when His people are hurting. In *Ecclesiastes 3*, God says there is a season for everything. In verse four it says "A time to weep, and a time to laugh, a time to mourn, and time to dance."

Grieving the loss of the life you expected for your child is normal. Grieving the extra challenges in your life and your child's is also normal. Grieving doesn't mean you love your child any less. In fact, I think it demonstrates just how much you cherish your child.

Once you fully accept, and even embrace your child's diagnosis, it doesn't mean the grief will suddenly disappear. There will be waves of grief on this journey. Things will be fine, life is looking good, and something will pop up that will trigger grief. Maybe it's watching a child effortlessly do what your child cannot. Or watching a parent do what you always dreamed of doing with your child. Or getting the results from an evaluation and seeing just how far behind your child is. Or watching your child struggle. Grief is healthy.

But it becomes unhealthy if we let the grief linger too long, if we let it keep us from moving on and taking care of our families like we need to. Unhealthy grief can lead us into a pit of anger or depression.

Grief should lead us to our knees before God, as it did for David, Mary, and Martha. You can turn to God in your grief and find strength and healing from God (we'll learn more about this in the next chapter) or you turn away from Him. If we don't turn toward God and instead distance ourselves from God and God's plan, then it becomes an unhealthy grief that leads to anger, bitterness, or depression.

Releasing Anger

David was now in great danger because all his men were very bitter about losing their sons and daughters, and they began to talk of stoning him. But David found strength in in the Lord his God (1 Samuel 30:6).

Remember that phrase, "Hurt people hurt people?" Here it is in action. David seemed like a prime target for his men's anger. Not the Ammorites who took their families, but David, simply because it was his idea to create and honor an alliance with the Philistines and they were not with their families.

I was taking a discipleship class with an amazing ministry a few months after we received my older son's diagnosis. One of the first assignments the teacher had us do was look over a list of sins we were to "put off," a list of godly characteristics we were to "put on," and a few verses to look up about each. I jumped into the assignment, ready to get my heart pure before God. Listed in alphabetical order, anger and bitterness stopped me in my tracks.

I had no idea I had such anger and bitterness embedded in my heart. We were supposed to spend a month going through this list of sins, but I never made it past the letter B. I spent a month parked in *Ephesians 4*, learning how detrimental anger was and how to release it.

Ephesians 4:26-27, "In your anger, do not sin: Do not let the sun go down while you are still angry, and do not give the devil a foothold." Ephesians 4:31-32, "Get rid of all bitterness, rage and anger ... Be kind and compassionate to one another, forgiving each other, just as in Christ God forgave you."

I was reminded of Naomi and her daughter-in-law Ruth, two women who lost their husbands and found themselves traveling back to Naomi's homeland together. Naomi was so bitter about the loss of her husband and sons that she told the people to call her Mara, which means *bitter*. "Don't call me Naomi. Call me Mara, because the Almighty has made my life very bitter. I went away full, but the Lord has brought me back empty" (*Ruth 1:20-21*).

In their culture, names were chosen not based on how the name sounds, but on its meaning. Although I cannot imagine losing your husband and your children, wanting to be called bitter is pretty extreme.

I recognized that feeling of bitterness Naomi felt in my own heart. And I didn't want it. I wanted to have faith to move forward as Ruth did, rather than marinating in anger and bitterness as Naomi did.

I confessed my bitterness to God. I shared with Him how I was feeling. And though He didn't say anything profound to me, I felt a peace I hadn't in a long time.

Any hurt or anger you are experiencing needs to be released. It doesn't matter if it's directed to God or someone else. It doesn't matter if it is even related to this special needs journey. It could be someone who hurt you years before you even became a mother. Regardless of who it is you are angry with, it isn't doing any good stuffed in your heart. In fact, it's hurting you, keeping you from the freedom and victory God wants in your life. It may take lots of time in prayer, honestly confessing to God how we feel before we can let go of the anger and find forgiveness, but it is worth it.

Releasing Pain

While David's men were focused on their inner pain and anger, David determined to focus on God. And once he found strength in the Lord, he knew he needed to take action. But he was going to do it God's way, not his own way.

> Then David said to Abiathar the priest, "Bring me the ephod." Abiathar brought it to him, and David inquired of the Lord, "Shall I pursue this raiding party? Will I overtake them?"
>
> "Pursue them," he answered. "You will certainly overtake them and succeed in the rescue" (1 Samuel 30:7-8).

I love that David asked God what to do. And then he immediately does what God says. There is no hesitation, just simple obedience. David takes his own army of four hundred men to go down to the Amalekites.

> David fought them from dusk until the evening of the next day, and none of them got away, except four hundred young men who rode off on camels and fled. David recovered everything the Amalekites had taken, including his two wives. Nothing was missing: young or old, boy or girl, plunder or anything else they had taken. David brought everything back. He took all the flocks and herds, and his men drove them ahead of the other livestock, saying "This is David's plunder" (1 Samuel 30:17-20).

God could have done anything to get those families restored. Instead God tells them to go to war. War is devastating. It changes the landscape of a country. It inflicts wounds and takes lives. And sometimes, that is exactly what this special needs journey feels like. A fight for every developmental milestone and every inch in between. A battle with insurance companies, specialists, and schools to get the services our children need.

Beth Moore says in her book *David, Seeking A Heart Like His*:

> "God often gives us a victory that requires blood, sweat, and tears. Why? Because He is practical. When He can bring about a victory and strengthen and mature us all at the same time, He's likely to do it. ... You see, God's idea of victory has virtually nothing to do with plunder. It has to do with people. What comes out of a battle isn't nearly as important as who comes out of a battle. That day, God not only worked a victory through David, but he also worked one in David. The man after God's own heart came out of battle with grace and mercy and a little better grasp of God's sovereignty. God gave him the opportunity to participate firsthand in the fight." (emphasis mine). [2]

Oh, how encouraging to know that there is a purpose in this! A plan to strengthen and mold us into the women, wives, and mothers God wants us to be. It was just after this battle that David was crowned king. This was the final preparation he needed to be ready to reign.

Now, you would think that would be the end of the story. They experienced pain, but yay, victory is theirs! Victory is ours! But there's one more emotion these men experienced. And I definitely can relate to this one!

Releasing Envy

Four hundred men went with David to the battle. But there were two hundred men who remained behind because "they were too exhausted to cross the valley" (verse 10). So when the four hundred bloodied, dirtied, exhausted, but victorious men returned with all their wives, children, and plunder and saw the two hundred men sitting around guarding their supplies, they suddenly didn't feel like sharing. They said

"Because they did not go out with us, we will not share with them the plunder we recovered. However, each man may take his wife and children and go."

David replied, "No, my brothers, you must not do that with what the Lord has given us. He has protected us and delivered into our hands the raiding party that came against us. Who will listen to what you say? The share of the man who stayed with the supplies is to be the same as that of him who went down to the battle. All will share alike" (1 Samuel 30:22-24).

I can understand the warriors' attitudes. I've been jealous of those parents who don't have to work hard for each and every new skill their child gains, but instead get to show off videos on Facebook of their kids singing songs at age two and riding a two-wheeled bike effortlessly at age four. It doesn't feel fair at all. It makes me want to say something that might end up fracturing our friendship. Or it makes me want to distance myself from them, feeling like we no longer have anything in common.

I've left playdates crying or avoided them altogether because I could see just how far behind my children are from their peers (or even children years younger than my own). And it made me envious of those mothers who were able to sit and chat and talk about random stuff, while I spent the entire time running around making sure my children didn't hurt other kids or hurt themselves.

Jealousy is a tool Satan uses to keep people from being in community, and community is something we desperately need.

Jealousy in and of itself is hard to release. The feelings will spring up whenever we see another child doing something we wish our child could do, or when we see a mother mothering the way we wish we could, or we see someone doing or having something we wish we could do or have.

But what we can control is our response. We can choose to be kind even if we are feeling jealous.

Healing the Gaping Hole

These four emotions, grief, anger, pain, and envy, form the acrostic GAPE. And a gape is a wide-open hole. These emotions are all natural, but if left to linger long enough will lacerate your heart. Perhaps that is why terms like heartbroken, heartrending, crushed, shattered, and devastated are used when a person feels some of these emotions. We can't heal these gaping holes ourselves. Only God can. And He longs to bring healing to our broken hearts. We'll learn a lot more about this in the next chapter.

Reflection Questions

1. Which of the four emotions (unhealthy grief, anger, pain, or envy) have you been struggling with the most?

2. Have you been responding more like David or like David's men to the events in your life? What can you do to respond more like David?

3. Are you experiencing anger and/or bitterness toward God or people in your life? If yes, what steps do you need to take to release the anger and seek reconciliation?

4. Pick a battle that was difficult for you, but God brought victory out of it. What has God accomplished in you as you battled through that difficult circumstance?

5. Has envy impacted you and your relationships with others? What steps can you take to respond in love when you are feeling jealous?

Chapter 3

Embracing God

A few years ago, I was experiencing an unusually exhausting day. My children were being more whiny and disobedient than usual. My younger son had decided that biting his older brother was his new way of defending himself. I spent over an hour on the phone with a doctor's office and insurance and still hadn't gotten an issue resolved. I got pulled over for speeding while heading to a therapy appointment. At the appointment, my son had a meltdown and his therapist wasn't able to work with him. I was tired and frustrated and I raged at God, "Where are you in all of this? Why aren't you helping?"

I desperately wanted to be alone with God, but the kiddos needed dinner and attention. And then, bedtime rolled around. After my older son, about four or five years old at the time, was all snuggled in bed and we had read his book before bed, we prayed together. Sometimes I did the praying, sometimes I did it fill in the blank style as he could only say one or two-word phrases. I decided to go with the fill-in-the-blank prayer.

> Me: "Thank you God for ____."
> "Eesus!" he said with a grin.

I choked back tears as I told him, "Yes, thank you God for Jesus." It was the first sign that he understood anything relating to God, Jesus, or Bible stories except for identifying "baby Eesus" at Christmas time. I've never prayed before using the words, "Thank you God for Jesus." It was his own spontaneous thought and it filled my heart with hope and joy.

We finished our prayers, I kissed that precious little guy goodnight, and as I left his room it hit me: God had answered my angry prayers through the mouth of my speech delayed child. I had demanded God tell me where He was and why it felt like He wasn't caring for us. And He gently reminded me He loved me and my children so much He gave us Jesus.

Oh, how amazing, how incredible is that? Though things may be rough, I am so thankful that God sent me His son Jesus to give me strength for all I need to do, to give me peace when I'm feeling overwhelmed, and to forgive my sin, anger, and frustration.

And as if that reminder that Jesus died for us because of God's love wasn't enough, a new thought hit me. God loved Jesus too. Because Jesus was His precious son.

After his baptism, Jesus came up out of the water and the heavens were opened and he saw the Spirit of God descending like a dove and settling on him. And a voice from heaven said, "This is my dearly loved Son, who brings me great joy" (Matthew 3:16-17).

And I realized that means God knows what it's like to see your own child suffer and struggle. He watched people not understand His son, watched them mock and test His son. He witnessed His child get beaten and whipped, carry a heavy wooden cross, and then have nails hammered through His wrists and ankles pinning Him to that cross. His son suffered for hours, and I'm sure God longed to take His son off of that cross, to hold Him tight in His arms, and take His beloved, innocent son far away from the cross. But He had a plan, He knew there was a glorious purpose in it. I'm sure that didn't make the pain and helplessness any less for Him though. His love for His son was still as strong as ever, but His love for you and me and for our children kept Him going with the plan.

He understands our pain when we watch our children go through medical procedures. He knows what it's like to watch our children struggle and long to change the circumstances for our children, but helpless to do so because we know it's ultimately for the best. He fully understands our pain when we see our children not be understood by others or mocked and excluded by others.

But He also sees the plan in it when we can't—a goodness that may benefit others more than we will ever understand or glimpse this side of eternity.

My prayer that night was "Thank you God, for "Eesus." And thank you God, that you understand my struggles and have promised to always be with me.""

Embracing God's Love for Our Children

One day, my older son had to be taken to the ER because he had an allergic reaction while at his preschool. He had never had an allergic reaction before. Ever.

After hearing the news I was surprisingly calm. I grabbed the kids' tablets, drinks, snacks for our wait in the ER, plus a few other essentials, and off my younger son and I sped to the hospital. I called my husband and cried, but after that phone call, I went back into calm, collected mama bear mode. It wasn't until that night, armed with an epi pen (just in case) that the fear and emotions took over. I sat in my son's bedroom, watching the reassuring rise and fall of his chest, imagining what would have happened if his teacher hadn't noticed his hives when she did, or if the school nurse hadn't given him the epi pen injection when he started having trouble breathing. Or what would happen if he had another reaction and I wasn't around.

Then, as worried mamas are known to do, I turned to Google. I read about allergy tests, symptoms, and reviews for the allergist we had an appointment with three weeks away. Anything could happen in those three weeks, right? I had to be prepared.

While my family slept peacefully, I researched and worried and wondered where God was in this new development.

And once I finally realized the fear was overtaking me and would mean I would never get to sleep, I abandoned Dr. Google and turned to God. And He, being much wiser and more loving than Google, led me to a verse I desperately needed and keep tucked in my heart.

> He tends his flock like a shepherd:
> he gathers the lambs in his arms
> and carries them close to his heart;
> he gently leads those that have young (Isaiah 40:11).

Tears flowed as I thanked God for loving my children more than I ever could and for holding them close to His heart. I was so thankful that He leads me, for I needed His wisdom, guidance, and strength in caring for these lambs He has entrusted to me. No matter the outcome of the allergy test, God held my precious son close to His heart, not just that day he had an allergic reaction, but every day.

Jesus longed to hold the children close as well.

Then people brought their children to Jesus for him to place his hands on them and pray for them. But the disciples rebuked them. Jesus said, 'Let the little children come to me, and do not hinder them, for the kingdom of heaven belongs to such as these' (*Matthew 19:13-15*).

In a culture where children were considered a blessing to their parents but a nuisance to others, Jesus demonstrated they were special and deserved blessing, closeness, touch, and love. He taught them children have a significant role, and He made them feel that way.

And the same is true for each of your precious lambs. He loves them more than we ever will, and we know we love them fiercely. He has a heart for them that we will never grasp this side of heaven, and it makes this mama heart of mine smile to know my Savior loves my children so fiercely.

He is holding them close when I cannot.

Embracing God's Wisdom

It's easy for us to ask God questions about suffering and our children and their special needs. Sometimes, we may ask God "Why my child? Why haven't you healed him yet? Why me? Why?"

One day, after months and months of pleading these questions and God not giving me an answer, I felt strongly God was telling me I'd been asking the wrong question.

"What other question is there?" I asked. I didn't get an answer right away, but when it came, it shifted my perspective. The question to ask was not *why?* but *what?* with a heart to learn God's heart.

For example, "What do you want me to learn from this journey? What good do you want to come from this? What testimony will we have from this? What do you want me to do to help my child? In what areas do I need to trust you more?" On and on, the questions went.

He'd never answered one of my *why* questions, but He started answering those *what* questions. Because He wanted me to grow stronger through this journey, to trust Him in ways I've never had to trust Him in before. Because He wanted me to encourage other moms going through the same journey. Because He would give me and my children an amazing testimony. Because He was growing in us a compassion for others. Because He was giving each member of our family a strength to persevere we wouldn't have had otherwise. Because we were growing closer to God than we would have without this journey we were going through. It may not always feel fair, but to know there's a reason and a purpose in it helps my heart tremendously.

Scripture indicates God's way of thinking is totally different than our own. By asking *what* questions instead of *why*, it puts God back on His throne. Asking *what* questions suggests humility, trusting God. Asking *why* suggests a hostility toward God, a belief that we know better than the Creator Himself. Ouch.

It's not wrong to ask God questions. Job and David asked God several questions when they were suffering or felt like they had been abandoned by God. And yet God loved those men very much. He called Job righteous and David a man after His own heart. He didn't always answer their questions, but He did let them know He was in control and understood things they could not.

We just need to make sure when we're asking questions, we ask them in humility, acknowledging God is sovereign, and we trust His answer.

Embracing God's Plan

Remember Ruth, who we discussed in the last chapter? She lost her husband and instead of wallowing in self-pity, chose to honor her mother-in-law and God by moving to her mother-in-law's homeland. And to glean in the fields, the only job available to widows without someone to care for them.

So Ruth woke up every morning to provide for the two of them. She worked harder than the other gleaners, picking up the left-over wheat the workers missed. She persevered and she maintained a positive attitude and people noticed her character.

Boaz in particular noticed. And that's where the story takes a beautiful turn. One in which Boaz eventually takes Ruth to be his wife. And they have a son together. And I'm sure Ruth kept on keeping on, doing what she did best. She worked hard to provide a clean, happy home for her husband, mother-in-law and son. She cooked meals and lent a hand to those in the community who needed help. That was her spirit, her character, her heart.

We make a big deal about how Ruth was rewarded for her faithfulness by becoming the great-great grandmother of King David and eventually the Messiah. And it is awesome. But, I don't think she ever got to see that happen in her lifetime. She saw that He provided her with a kind husband and then blessed her with a son after having a previous childless marriage. She saw that God's hand was upon her, providing for her, but she didn't see the whole picture. She didn't see that her descendants would include the great King David and the Savior of the world.

And to be honest, I find that encouraging. Sure, I want to know what God's plan is for my life and my childrens' lives. I want to know exactly how my children having special needs brings God glory. But, what I find encouraging is simply that all I have to do is keep on keeping on. Keep on taking care of my family. Keep on loving God and being obedient to Him. And something good and beautiful will happen. Now, yes, I want to see it happen in my lifetime. But if it doesn't, I'm learning to be ok with that. According to *Romans 8:28*, we know that "He works all things together for those who love Him." I've seen Him work things out for His glory throughout the Bible. He did it for Ruth. He'll do it for me. He'll do it for you. That's just who He is, and I'm glad that His plan and His goal is to "make all things beautiful in its time. He has also set eternity in the human heart, yet no one can fathom what God has done from beginning to end" (*Ecclesiastes 3:11*).

Embracing God's Healing

There is a story in the Bible that I love embedded in *Mark 5*. Verses 24-34 tell the story of a woman who had been suffering a bleeding issue for twelve years.

This woman was not only physically unwell–imagine the weakness that comes from a ceaseless menstrual flow for twelve years without iron supplements, imagine the continual cleansing of clothes and self–but she was also considered culturally unclean. According to the laws in *Leviticus 15:19-30*, she was to remain away from other people so they would not be unclean. A law meant to protect the people from unsanitary conditions when there were no pads or tampons, became one that caused the culture to judge and isolate her from friends and family for over a decade.

Like this woman, I have felt isolated from friends and family because of this special needs journey. They don't understand what our journey is like. We don't have the time or energy to meet with others. Sometimes there's even a little bit of shame involved, as the public can see the differences in our children and we feel called out or avoided because of it.

So, for twelve years she does all she can to help herself. She hires doctors who I'm sure tried lots of different solutions, but all that resulted in was a dwindling of funds. I can relate to this too. We've spent thousands of dollars taking our children to specialists and therapists to get them the help they needed. We've tried different supplements and diets reported to help. We even built a ball pit in our boy's room to help them with their sensory and gross motor issues. I get the desperation for health and wellness. I also get the depression that can set in when you feel there is no hope.

But then she heard Jesus was coming to town. She heard about others who were healed. A glimmer of hope! And since she knew she couldn't be seen in public, she would have to hide under a shawl, keep her head down, and simply touch his cloak. She believed it would be enough. She had faith. And she was willing to risk everything to act on it.

I can only imagine the joy she felt when she managed to make it to Jesus unnoticed, reached out to touch His cloak, and immediately felt healing and strength course through her body. The freedom she experienced—realizing she was no longer unclean, that she could return to her family and friends, that she could go back in the temple and pray with the other women.

I'm sure it was to her absolute horror that Jesus stopped and turned around and asked "Who touched me?" She likely dropped back, trying to hide, to blend in. Surely He would just think someone bumped into Him. That's what His disciples told him. At least, I think that's how I would have responded. In a culture where you don't touch a man unless you are related or married to him, and definitely don't touch anyone when you are unclean, I don't think I would have confessed what I'd done, no matter how joyful I was to be healed. But I have lots of wimpy faith moments, and for this woman it was a moment of faith, courage, boldness, and humility.

This woman, a shamed outcast for twelve years, boldly stepped forward, fell to her knees with humility, and confessed. Verse 33 says she told him "the whole truth." I imagine this means she didn't just admit she was the one to touch Him, but she told him about her shameful disorder, about her suffering, about how she'd strived for healing for twelve years and finally found it by touching His cloak.

She had embraced that He could heal her. He did. Now, she embraced the hope that He would have mercy on her and not add to her shame.

And then He calls her daughter. Daughter! How beautiful! She had come to Jesus to find healing from her suffering, and Jesus embraced her into His family, making her not only culturally acceptable again, but intimately connected to Him.

And God does the same to us. He knows every tear we have cried. He sees the hemorrhaging in our own hearts, the gaping holes our pain and anger and grief and envy have caused. And He reaches out and embraces us, just as we are. He stops the bleeding with just a touch. He restores our identity with just a word. "Daughter."

And then He tells her to "go in peace and be freed from all your suffering" (v 34). Her body was healed just by reaching out to Him in faith. Her heart was healed of the wounds and shame she had carried for twelve years.

We need to go before God and tell Him everything. Tell Him every wound in our hearts and how we've tried to heal them ourselves but can't. How much we need a touch from Him. Sometimes I think it's hard to do, because we feel He already knows what's going on in our hearts. But that doesn't mean He doesn't want to hear it from us. He wants us to approach Him and share with Him what we're feeling and thinking, even if it scares us or we're mad at Him. I'll admit, I've approached Him before and told Him I was mad at Him or disappointed with Him. And I leave those conversations feeling God's love for me again. Feeling like I am His daughter and He cares about my concerns and my suffering. Feeling again like He is for me.

I encourage you, to sit before God and be honest with Him. Pour out your words and tears. Write God a letter if it's easier for you; I've done that many times. And then leave that precious time feeling relieved that He still cares for you and your child(ren) more than you will ever grasp or understand. That He is holding you and your child(ren) in the palm of His hands. That He embraces you when you embrace Him and His love for you.

Reflection Questions

1. Does knowing that God is familiar with parenting a child with unique struggles, needs, and giftings make it easier to embrace God?

2. How has God demonstrated His love to you and your child(ren) recently or in the past?

3. What kind of questions have you been asking God? Have you been asking them with a demanding or humble attitude?

4. Do you find Ruth not knowing all of God's plan encouraging, or discouraging? Why?

5. What kind of healing does your heart need now? Share with God your wounds and your worries until you feel God's peace and presence in your life, and truly know, deep in your heart, that you are His beloved "Daughter."

Chapter 4

Releasing Plans

I was a middle school English teacher before I became a mom, and I taught several special need students. I loved each and every one of my students, but I honestly disliked going to IEP meetings. When I decided to stop teaching to be a stay at home mom, I never expected I'd have to go to another IEP meeting, let alone that I'd be sitting on the other side of the table of an IEP meeting as a parent. And I especially didn't expect that I'd be on the parent side of the table for two children with IEPs.

As an extrovert with several friends and sisters-in-law all having babies around the same time I was, I dreamed of playdates and birthday parties and drinking coffee together, boasting about our children. I didn't expect that I'd cry in my car on the way home from play dates because my child was so far behind his peers. And I definitely didn't expect that before long I'd avoid friends and play dates altogether.

I had dreams of homeschooling my children. I was an educator, after all. I had Pinterest boards filled with homeschooling ideas and tips. But when my older son turned five, we thought he might do better in an environment where he could learn from his peers, where there would be more structure than I could give him, and where he could get therapies our insurance wasn't covering. I never expected to put my kids on the school bus and let someone else teach them. And I never in a million years expected they would ride to school on a special needs bus with an aide and seat belts.

Nothing was going in my life as I expected, and it led me to a crisis of faith that scared me. Did God even exist? I sure wasn't seeing Him in my life or my kids' lives. If He did exist, was God good like I'd always believed? He sure didn't feel like a good Father to me.

One Christmas season, while rereading the all-too-familiar story from the first two chapters of Luke, I felt God gave me fresh eyes and I experienced the story from Mary's perspective, restoring my faith in God's goodness again.

Releasing Our Expectations

We know little about Mary's personality, her thoughts, her reactions, or her dreams, so I'm going to share with you my interpretation of what I think the mother of our Savior may have been thinking and experiencing. As a former teen girl, I'm positive she daydreamed about having a loving husband, of having children (especially sons in their culture), and being a good wife and mother. I doubt she had huge dreams for her life, but she envisioned it with love and marriage before the baby carriage.

And she was on track to having those dreams come true when she becomes betrothed to Joseph. Then an angel showed up. This wasn't a cute, little Precious Moments angel sporting a lopsided halo. When every single biblical character who sees an angel falls on their face and the angel has to tell them to "Fear not," or "Be not afraid," I'm pretty sure they're a lot more terrifying than we depict them in nativities.

But this time, the angel didn't start with his "don't be afraid" speech. He sent her greetings and told her she was highly favored. No wonder this poor girl was "greatly troubled" (*Luke 1:29*). She had no idea why this mighty being was before her, but it said she was favored.

The angel filled her in in verses 31-33. She was going to conceive and give birth to the Messiah. This was something that I'm sure all Jewish girls and mothers longed for, to bring the long-awaited Savior into the world. She must have felt both overwhelmed and honored. She simply asked one question and was satisfied with the answer. I'm sure I would have had hundreds!

Or I would have been like so many of the famous Bible characters who all made up an excuse about why they weren't qualified for the job. I probably would have said no thank you, I don't want to be accused of adultery and stoned, find someone who is married to bear the Messiah. I probably would have come up with excuses after I asked my plethora of questions.

But not Mary. In verse 38 she said, "I am the Lord's servant," and "May your word to me be fulfilled."

Mary's pregnancy would change her life, her status, her reputation, and her marriage (if it still was going to happen). It would change everything. She accepted that she was merely a servant of the Lord and ready to do as He asked of her.

Joseph almost divorces her, and I'm sure she was rejected and ridiculed by the people in her community. Maybe even by her family. This was a full-fledged scandal.

But what did she do? She didn't complain or get angry at her plans going unmet. Nope, she found someone in a similar situation, a relative named Elizabeth who was also expecting a baby under a similar miraculous circumstance, and instead of complaining or voicing fears and concerns, they both praised God for choosing them. That He had blessed them. That He would bless every person through the child Mary is carrying.

How I wish I could praise God rather than accuse Him of not doing what I think is good.

When things finally seem to settle down, God gave her unexpected circumstance number two. She would have to travel to Bethlehem to register for the tax while pregnant. And have the baby there, far away from her friends and family who normally assisted with a birth.

I was in this place when my second son was born. We had just moved to a new state a few weeks before he was born. It was lonely. Overwhelming. Stressful. And I was a little bitter at my husband and at God for the circumstances surrounding it. But we catch no glimpse of that with Mary. She rode a donkey thousands of miles while hugely pregnant. No air conditioning and reclining seats and fast food drive-thrus. No hotels.com to book their hotels in advance. No Google to find a midwife in Bethlehem available to deliver her baby.

And then, unexpected circumstance number three. She went into labor, and the only place they could find for her to have the baby was the stable. There was no midwife, not even her mother or another woman to support her through her labor and delivery. Pretty sure this is not how Mary imagined giving birth.

Releasing Our Way

I wonder if when all this happened, Mary questioned if she had heard God right. I mean, how could this possibly be God's plan, for the Messiah to be born to a virgin teenager in a smelly stable peppered with animal poop? And I don't know, maybe the hormonal Mary did cry at the circumstances surrounding this birth. Maybe she did question if she had heard God right, or if this really was the Savior of the world, why God would let him to come into the world this way. Or maybe she simply yielded to God's plan and marveled at the Christ child sleeping peacefully in the manger, as we depict in our nativities.

I don't know what went on in Mary's head or heart, but God encouraged her by what happened next in *Luke 2:8-20*. The shepherds came and told Mary and Joseph they had seen angels announcing the "Savior, the Messiah, the Lord has been born." How much awe and wonder that must have brought to this young couple, in the middle of nowhere with no friends or family to celebrate with them.

Verse 19 says "Mary treasured up all these things and pondered them in her heart." Oh, how I wish I pondered and treasured the things of God in my life, like Mary. Instead, I tend to start focusing on how life isn't unfolding the way I would have planned it to, or get overwhelmed with my to-do list and what I should do next.

I think one of the reasons Mary had such a yielded heart is because she knew her place. She was God's servant. She even told the angel so.

Sometimes we forget our place, forget God is in control and is sovereign, and it's easy to get upset when things don't go our way. When we get a diagnosis, or a surprise trip to the ER, or whatever unexpected event life throws our way.

But we need to stop being so focused on *our way* and start being followers of *the Way*. That's what the early Christians called themselves, followers of the Way. They knew that following God, no matter what persecutions they were to endure, was what mattered.

That means we need to stop with all the thinking, planning, worrying, controlling and instead live in the moment. Embrace what's in front of us. Embrace the journey we are on and the ways we are growing on the journey. Embrace every blessing in our life and treasure it in our heart. No, it's not easy, but it's the easiest way to experience God's peace and joy in our lives.

In fact, let's look at the angels' words to the shepherds in *Luke 2:14.* "Glory to God in the highest, and *peace* on earth to those with whom his favor rests."

Did you catch the part where it says there is peace for those on "whom his favor rests"? It was on Mary when the angel told her she was favored and going to be the mother of the Messiah. Favor is on us too.

Mary's life was challenging. She raised a child that was without sin—pretty sure there were no support groups for that. At some point, she became a widow. She watched her beloved child get rejected by the people of their town. She heard people talk of killing her son. There were times she was reminded that He was more powerful than she, and she no longer had authority over him. And there was that heartbreaking time she witnessed her innocent son suffer a humiliating and excruciating death on a cross.

I doubt she felt favored then. I can't even imagine the sorrow. But I think what got her through those horrific times was that she clung to those treasures she had embedded in her heart thirty-three years before. She knew her son was the Savior of the world and it kept her going, kept her trusting God and His plan for the world.

You can embrace God's plan, even if it's different than you expected. You can ponder it like Mary did, praise Him for giving you the opportunity to be part of it.

Or you can keep holding on to your expectations and the bitterness, sadness, worry, fear, and anger that come from unmet expectations from God. I believe Mary accepted the circumstances she couldn't change regarding the Savior's arrival, and she experienced peace and beauty in being the mother of this precious child and a servant of the Lord God Almighty. It may not have made sense, but it was beautiful and praiseworthy to all who witnessed the Savior of the world lying peacefully in the manger.

According to *Acts 1:13-15*, Mary was there in that upper room when the Holy Spirit fell on them. Mary, who had experienced her fair share of trials and struggles and unmet expectations, who had buried her Son and then held Him in her arms again alive, and then watched Him disappear into heaven, also got to experience the fullness of the promises of God flowing in her life. She saw it flow in the lives of those around her, those lives that were touched by her Son. And I'm sure she treasured those things in her heart for the rest of her life.

If you are having a tough time embracing God's plan rather than your own plans, I highly recommend you listen to the song "Thy Will" by Hillary Scott. The first time I heard this song I sobbed as I realized I wasn't trusting God's plans and was instead focusing on my own expectations and feelings regarding them. I listened to it again, tears still falling. The third time I found I could sing along, truly believing the words I was singing. A peace filled my heart as I released how I wanted my life to go and instead embraced God's will for my life and for my children. I often listen to this song because I need the reminder to trust God's will and His way.

Mary essentially told God, "Thy will be done." Thirty-three years later, her son taught people to pray: "Thy kingdom come, *thy will be done*, on earth as it is in heaven" (*Matthew 6:10*). He said "Thy will be done" before going to the cross (*Luke 22:42*). It is hard to surrender our own plans and expectations as we trust His. We may need to work on this daily, but it is so worth it when we can ponder with acceptance and even joy the things God is doing in our lives.

Reflection Questions

1. How do you usually react when an expectation you had goes unmet?

2. In what way would you like to respond a little more like Mary when God's plans differ from your own?

3. What can you praise God for in your life? In this special needs journey?

4. What has God been teaching you through the unexpected circumstances in your life?

5. How would embracing the circumstances in your life as

part of God's plan and purpose for you help you experience peace?

Chapter 5

Embracing Perseverance

"V-I-C-T-O-R-Y. Victory! Victory! That's our cry!"

Such are the words chanted by D-Bob in the 1993 inspirational movie, *Rudy*. Rudy was determined to see his dream come true: to play football for Notre Dame. The obstacles that came upon him, the teasing and opposition from family members and friends, and his own small stature couldn't keep him from striving toward that victory he longed to experience. He worked for years to make enough money to go to a community college, and had to work multiple jobs to stay in school. He worked hard in his classes, despite his dyslexia, so he could get accepted to Notre Dame. He worked out constantly. He received his fair share of rejection letters from Notre Dame. And when he got knocked down, bloodied, and bruised, (literally or figuratively) he'd pop right back up again, ready for more.

Sure, he wanted to give up from time to time. But he always remembered his life's dream and worked for it. All he wanted was to play on the Notre Dame football field in a game. That cheer that Rudy's best friend D-Bob cried wasn't just a random school cheer for Rudy, it was a way of life for him.

It wouldn't have been an interesting movie if Rudy had said "I'm going to play football for Notre Dame," immediately made the team, scored hundreds of touchdowns, and faced no struggles or obstacles.

The reason I love that movie so much is because I love Rudy's determination and his growth as he faces his struggles. I love watching him become stronger, not just physically, but mentally, spiritually, and in character. And I can't help but grin when I see him succeed despite all the obstacles. Because he worked so hard for his victory, it must have tasted that much sweeter. A victory he could savor forever.

Embracing Peace in the Struggles

Of all the characters in the Bible who faced their share of struggles and persevered despite them, Paul is a stand-out.

Paul was born a Roman citizen, which required four generations of living in Rome and being able to offer something of value to Rome, the wealthiest city in that time. Being a Roman citizen entitled him to many rights, including a fair trial if arrested and the right to appeal it if he didn't like the outcome. Though born in Rome and qualifying for Roman citizenship, he was raised in Jerusalem, the Holy City, the city where all Jews longed to live or at least visit at least once in their lifetime. The Jewish citizens who were able to observe feasts and contribute sacrifices throughout the year at the temple in Jerusalem were given the status of Orthodox Jew, and Orthodox Jews could then become a Pharisee or Sadducee, with a Pharisee having highest standing. Paul was taught by Gamaliel, one of the most prominent rabbis of that time, receiving a broad education not only in religion but also ethics, literature, logic, and several languages including Greek, Hebrew, and Aramaic. Paul became a Pharisee, which meant he not only followed the Jewish religion to the letter, but it entitled him to look down on those who did not. Life was pretty good for him. He was wealthy and powerful and well educated and had prominent status.

But then Paul experiences an event that changes his life. Recorded in *Acts 9:1-9*, Saul (who would later be renamed Paul) was traveling to Damascus with plans to arrest any followers of the Way. He was blindsided–knocked to the ground by the power of God, told to stop persecuting Jesus by persecuting the followers of the Way. Blinded.

He no longer knew what he was supposed to do, only that he was to wait. And he was unable to eat or drink for three days.

Once God restored sight to Paul again, his life changed. His purpose changed. He went from persecuting and killing Christians to living with them, teaching them, risking his life for them.

I can relate to a lot of what happened to Saul/Paul. My life was pretty good, filled with a supportive husband, close friends, a church we loved, and a precious little baby I loved fiercely. And then we noticed things weren't exactly the way they should be with that precious baby. When he received his first diagnosis, I wasn't that devastated. It was easy to manage. Not terribly life-transforming. But when a second and then a third and fourth diagnosis arrived one right after the other, and then our second son received a few diagnoses of his own, I felt blindsided. Lost. Confused. Depressed and anxious.

This new life wasn't easy for Paul either. He left behind his old life, with power and position and the name Saul (which means "inquired for/asked of God" like King Saul from the Old Testament) and transformed into Paul (which means "humble or small"). The significance of the name change rippled through his life as he transformed from a mighty, powerful, prominent, and wealthy man into a lowly tentmaker working hard to feed himself and serve God. He experienced a lot of struggles. According to *2 Corinthians 11:24-28*:

> Five different times the Jewish leaders gave me thirty-nine lashes. Three times I was beaten with rods. Once I was stoned. Three times I was shipwrecked. Once I spent a whole night and a day adrift at sea. I have traveled on many long journeys. I have faced danger from rivers and from robbers. I have faced danger from my own people, the Jews, as well as the Gentiles. I have faced danger in the cities, in the deserts, and on the seas. And I have faced danger from men who claim to be believers but are not. I have worked hard and long, enduring many

> sleepless nights. I have been hungry and thirsty and have often gone without food. I have shivered in the cold, without enough clothing to keep me warm. Then, besides all this, I have the daily burden of my concern for all the churches.

While I'm happy to report I've never been beaten, whipped, stoned, adrift at sea for twenty-four hours, or robbed, I have had my own struggles. I can relate to working hard and long, his sleepless nights, and his daily burden of worry, though in my case it's for my children. I've struggled with anxiety, depression and health issues during this special needs journey. I'm sure you can think of struggles you've experienced.

Serving God was hard for Paul. It was no fun. But Paul found purpose in it which enabled him to persevere. He was willing to die for his faith and his Savior. He used his faith and his education and his experiences and became one of the best teachers and encouragers of the early church. His words have penned at least thirteen books of our Bible. Like a pebble dropped in still water, his faith spread to the disciples, entire churches, and has trickled down to us today. I think if he could see how his words and actions have impacted our culture today, almost two thousand years later, he would be amazed, and humbled, and give God all the glory.

While we tend to complain about the struggles we're going through and question God's goodness, Paul had a unique perspective on hardships and weaknesses. *In 2 Corinthians 12:7-11* he wrote:

To keep me from becoming proud, I was given a thorn in my flesh, a messenger from Satan to torment me and keep me from becoming proud.

Three different times I begged the Lord to take it away. Each time he said, "My grace is all you need. My power works best in weakness." So now I am glad to boast about my weaknesses, so that the power of Christ can work through me. That's why I take pleasure in my weaknesses, and in the insults, hardships, persecutions and troubles that I suffer for Christ. For when I am weak, then I am strong.

Honestly? The journey has not been fun. But when I take a step back from my emotions, I see a glimpse of the big picture. I don't have the whole picture, only God does, but here's the glimpse of the picture I see: God took a random middle school teacher with a tendency to avoid conflict and confrontation and called her to become a strong mama bear who would fiercely love, fight for, teach, and encourage her two special cubs. God took a woman who dreamed of writing and publishing young adult novels and told her instead to write a book to encourage fellow special needs moms. He took a woman struggling with anxiety, depression, loneliness, and exhaustion and taught her to release what didn't serve her or her family and to instead embrace life, to find victory in the little moments, to find joy in the blessings, and to celebrate the growth in her heart as much as the inchstones and milestones her children made. He took a woman who thought she could do everything in her own strength and made her lean on Him in ways she never had to before. Daily. In that light, the struggles are worth it. Still not fun, but there's a purpose in it, and the purpose makes it worth it to keep on persevering in faith.

Embracing Contentment Despite the Struggles

I read a passage in *Calm My Anxious Heart* by Linda Dillow (I highly recommend that book!) that transformed my view of how to persevere through the struggles. She describes a woman named Ella, a missionary in Africa for fifty-two years, who raised her family without the modern conveniences we enjoy, such as electricity, indoor plumbing, and of course, air conditioning. Here's what Linda Dillow says,

> Ella's daughter, Mimi, is my friend. Mimi wondered how her mother had done it—how she lived a life of contentment when her circumstances would have caused the hardiest to complain. Recently, Mimi unearthed a treasure, a much more significant find than gold or silver. In an old diary of her mother's she discovered Ella's prescription for contentment:
>
> - Never allow yourself to complain about anything—not even the weather.
> - Never picture yourself in any other circumstance or someplace else.
> - Never compare your lot with another's.
> - Never allow yourself to wish this or that had been otherwise.
> - Never dwell on tomorrow—remember that tomorrow is God's, not ours. [3]

Wow. I was so convicted when I read this. I am guilty of doing every single one of these, pretty much every single day. And I can see how being rooted in the present moment and in your present circumstances rather than in your struggles can bring a lot of contentment and peace to your mind and soul. How it can encourage you to keep persevering in faith, focused on the calling God has given you.

Linda Dillow then adds,

> Her eyes were fixed on eternity. Her tomorrows belonged to God. She had given them to Him. And because all her tomorrows were nestled in God's strong arms, she was free to live today. One day at a time she could make the right choices and grow to possess the holy habit of contentment. Ella's focus was eternal, and her focus led to an eternal contentment.

In a nutshell, she was able to persevere as a missionary in Africa for five decades because she chose to be at peace and enjoy what she had been given, rather than focus on the struggles and the things she wanted.

Contentedness seems to be the key. Paul learned this, too.

Paul wrote, in *Philippians 4:11-13*

> for I have learned to be content whatever the circumstances. I know what it is to be in need, and I know what it is to have plenty. I have learned the secret of being content in any and every situation, whether well fed or hungry, whether living in plenty or in want. I can

do everything through him who gives me strength.

This is a man who had been shipwrecked, beaten, persecuted, whipped, and was in prison while writing the letter that contained these lines. He decided to not focus on the circumstances and instead focus on God, who gave him the strength to persevere and do all things.

How does Paul do it? He tells us twice "I have learned." It was a process for him. It didn't come naturally. It was something he had to be intentional about, to make a priority in his life. I'm sure not complaining about the heat didn't come naturally to Ella. That's why she had to write down her prescription for contentment. She had to remind herself whenever she felt the urge to complain or to wish that she had a washing machine or dishwasher or air conditioning. It's a process we are fully capable of making in our own lives. And both Ella and Paul realized their strength to be content came from God.

Ultimately, peace and contentment come more from how we think about things rather than about how our circumstances change. We may want our circumstances to change, but dwelling on that will not lead to peace. By changing our perspective and focusing on all the things we have to be grateful for, we will experience peace and joy.

Reflection Questions

1. How has your life changed since becoming a special needs mother?

2. How has your relationship with God changed because of this journey? How would you like it to change?

3. What purpose do you think God might have for this special needs journey you are on?

4. What circumstances in your life have you not been content with?

5. How would being content in all circumstances allow you to experience peace and persevere in faith?

Chapter 6

Releasing Control

When my older son started to get diagnosis after diagnosis, I went into fierce mama bear mode.

I joined Facebook support groups for every one of his disorders (or suspected disorders). I read every book I could get my hands on about each of his diagnoses. I researched therapies, supplements, and toys that could help him learn. There were times I believed that maybe the next thing I found would be the magic bullet that would miraculously help my child.

I was all about getting anything that was supposed to help, no matter the cost. In my desperation I was ready to take my son half-way across the country to see the top specialist for his diagnosis, for a week-long 1-on-1 time with her that would cost a lot of money. I'd read the testimonials and just knew it would help my son too. But when I excitedly presented my findings to my husband, he told me that it wouldn't fit in our budget. Shocked that he didn't share my enthusiasm, I asked him if he cared about money more than our child, and an argument ensued.

After that argument, I stormed off to our master bedroom closet (definitely not one of my finest moments) to cry and process my emotions. As I sat in that closet, I cried out to God for help—wondering where He was in this situation and in my marriage.

And the passage of Mary and Martha from *Luke 10* popped into my mind.

The more I thought about Mary and Martha, the more I realized I had become like Martha, bustling about trying to do everything myself and getting mad that Mary (in this case God and my husband) wasn't helping like I wanted.

And in the process, I was missing out on enjoying my children for who they were. I was missing out on peace, joy, and thankfulness for the abundant blessings in my life. But mostly, I was missing out on time with God and trusting God, convinced it was up to me to help both my sons.

I was too busy to even hear the gentle rebuke, "You are worried and upset about many things, but few things are needed—or indeed, only one. Mary has chosen what is better, and it will not be taken away from her" (*Luke 10:41-42*).

I admitted to God I had held my children so closely I hadn't let Him have any control of their lives. I had let fears of their development and God not intervening in my childrens' lives like I wanted Him to, make me feel I had to be the one in control. I had focused so much on therapies and researching everything that could make things better for my boys, that I hadn't focused on my marriage, my relationship with God, or even just enjoyed being with my children.

I had believed I could sprint my boys to a finish line where all their disorders would be resolved within a few years, rather than accepting we were on a marathon and the finish line was nowhere in sight. I had to embrace the fact that my children might never be healed, but we needed to keep moving at a more realistic, steady pace. I had to exchange my exhausting frantic sprint for a balanced plan of action.

I had to trust God with my children. And I had to work as a teammate with my husband to figure out not only what was best for our children, but for our whole family as well, but we'll go into that more in our next chapter.

Releasing Our Children into God's Care

My older son had just turned five and could have started kindergarten, but I applied for him to attend a preschool for special needs children. It was an amazing school with equally amazing staff and miracle of miracles, he got in. They agreed that an extra year of preschool, especially one with the services they could offer, was exactly what he needed.

And so I dropped him off at his new school, was proud of myself for not crying, and went home with only my younger son to take care of. I worried about how he'd do. My heart ached to know he wouldn't be able to tell me what he had done all day or if he was making friends and I'd have to rely on teacher reports.

I prayed that God would take care of my son. That he would love school and learn and grow. And day by day, we watched it happen.

He was flourishing. New words. And then phrases. And then short sentences. More smiles and social interactions with other kids. Reading words and writing letters. He even developed his first friendship, and when I asked what he did with his new friend at school he told me with utter seriousness, "Play. Learn. Hold hands."

I had let my son go, and he was growing, and even had a girlfriend.

I was reminded of Hannah, who let her long-awaited son Samuel go, and he grew into the greatest prophet of Israel.

I was reminded of Moses' mother, who to protect her child, put him in a basket, let him go down a river (way scarier than off to a special needs preschool classroom!) and Moses grew into the man who would deliver the Israelites from slavery and into the Promised Land.

And I was reminded of Mary, who had to let her son go and become the Savior of the world.

Wow, were these mothers brave! They had no idea what would happen to their beloved sons. But they trusted God.

Was it easy for these biblical mothers? No way. I can't imagine how hard it was for these mamas to not be able to raise their children like they had dreamed of and wanted to. But they loved God and God's plan for their child more than their own desire to keep their children close and protected. Wow, is that powerful.

I'm not saying we let our kids go and be raised by our priests or pastors. I'm saying we hold our children in our open hands, trusting that God has a plan for them and we shouldn't get in the way of it. We shouldn't hold them so close that they can't fulfil what God has planned for them.

No, it's not easy, bravely letting our kids go. Bravely sending your child to the operating room for another surgery or watching your child undergo a medical procedure. Bravely sending him to another therapist to evaluate and work with your child. Bravely dropping her off at school. Bravely letting our children enter new environments where we're not sure how they'll do. It's a scary world for our children.

But we can't protect our children from everything. We're not meant to.

We need to entrust them into God's care. Trust that God will take care of them when we cannot.

If Hannah had clung to Samuel as if he was solely hers and Elkanah's, Samuel probably would not have grown up to be one of the greatest prophets of Israel.

If Moses's mother hadn't let her son go in basket down the river, Moses wouldn't have been able to free his people and lead them to the Promised Land.

And if Mary had held her son close to her, He would not have been able to lead a ministry that has changed our eternity and given us an abundant life.

Now, I don't want you to feel guilty for loving your children and protecting them. But my point is we need to be willing to release our children to God. To trust His will for them. To trust that He can take care of our children better than we can. That He has a bigger plan for our children than we do. That He loves them even more than we do.

I love the passage from *Isaiah 40:11*, "He will carry the lambs in his arms, holding them close to his heart. He will gently lead the mother sheep with their young."

The shepherd can only carry the lambs close to his heart if the mother lets him hold her lamb. If she trusts the shepherd can protect and love her lamb in ways she cannot. What a beautiful image—the God of the universe cradling our children close to His beating heart. And caring for us too.

If you have never released your children to God, or need to do so again, below is a beautiful prayer taken from the book *The Power of a Praying Parent,* by Stormie Omartian to help you.

Lord, I come to you in Jesus' name and give (name of child) to You. I'm convinced that You alone know what is best for him (her). You alone know what he (she) needs. I release him (her) to You to care for and protect, and I commit myself to pray for everything concerning him (her) that I can think of or that you put upon my heart ...

Thank you that I can partner with You in raising him (her) and that I don't have to do it alone. I'm grateful that I don't have to rely on the world's unreliable and ever-changing methods for child rearing, but that I can have clear directions from Your Word and wisdom as I pray to You for answers.

Thank you, Lord, for the precious gift of this child. Because Your Word says that every good and perfect gift comes from you, I know that You have given him (her) to me to care for and raise. Help me to do that. Show me places where I continue to hang on to him (her) and enable me to release him (her) to Your protection, guidance, and counsel. Help me not to live in fear of possible dangers, but in the joy and peace of knowing that You are in control. I rely on You for everything, and this day I trust my child to You and release him (her) into your hands. [4]

Bravely Allowing Our Children to Try New Things

I once watched a video on YouTube of a mother duck and her little ducklings jumping up a set of stairs. The mother duck of course hopped them effortlessly, and then waited for her children to follow. And so began their desperate attempt at hopping up steps twice as tall as they were. It took them a while before a few of the ducklings made it up the first step. Some still struggled with the first step, while others were working on the second step, and a few had gotten a hang of what they needed to do and effortlessly made it up the third step.

Except for one little duckling. It hadn't even made it up the first step while all of its siblings made it to the top. But the mother duck never moved, waiting for her last baby to make its way up the staircase. And though it would hop and fall back down, eventually it made it up that first step. A few attempts later it was up the second and then finally the third step. And the moment that last duckling made it all the way up, the mother waddled off, all her ducklings following behind her.

The comments on that video were all about persistence, not giving up, the bravery (and cuteness) of those little ducklings, especially the last one.

I was inspired and encouraged by those little ducklings. I was especially proud of that last little duckling for sticking with it, for not giving up. I saw my boys in that last little duckling, how they struggle and work hard, and eventually, in their own timing, succeed.

But honestly, I was captivated by that mother duck. And I realized how unlike that mother duck I was. I would have been thinking, *Oh, you can't climb the stairs yet. Let me show you how, and if you can't get it after a few attempts, we'll find another way to our destination and you can try the stairs a little bit later, when you're older, stronger, and taller. Maybe we can talk to the physical therapist about working on stair climbing in future sessions.*

Yes, sometimes I do more for my kids than I should because I'm impatient. We're in a hurry and I know I can do it faster. Other times I do things myself because I don't think my kids are ready for it, or I don't want to teach that skill right now. We have enough stuff we're trying to master now as it is, right? Other times it's just out of fear. Fear that my child can't do something and will get hurt or get discouraged.

But watching that mother duck made me realize how much I don't want my children to miss out on opportunities to grow in strength and independence and mastering essential life and self-help skills they should be able to do on their own one day. Why not try right now?

I want my children to be overcomers, not over-protected.

I'm reminded of the parents in both Finding Nemo and Finding Dory. Both Nemo's and Dory's parents are special needs parents. And they have different approaches to raising their children.

Nemo's dad Marlin is very fearful and overprotective, longing to keep Nemo close and afraid to let him try new things. At one point Marlin even tells Nemo, "You think you can do these things, Nemo, but you just can't!"

You can see the hurt in Nemo's face. If Nemo had believed his dad, there would be no Finding Nemo or Finding Dory. It would be a boring, lonely story of staying safe in their sea anemone home.

But Nemo was determined to try the things he knew he was capable of. And over time, Marlin bravely learned to give his son opportunities to try new things. To grow and learn on his own. To not hold him back because of his "lucky fin."

Dory's parents, Jenny and Charlie, also protect their child, but they know the best way they can protect her is to teach her strategies for remembering important information due to her "short term remembery loss." They could have kept her close, told her not to leave, as Marlin tried to, but they knew Dory needed to learn to stay safe and be able to find her way back home. And they clung to the hope that their daughter would be able to remember all they taught her.

When Dory eventually does find her way back home, using the methods her parents patiently taught her over and over again, they told her "You did it! You know what this means Dory? It means you can do anything!"

Ah, the power of encouragement. Of believing in your children and bravely encouraging them to try things on their own. Of not limiting them because of a diagnosis or disability.

Who knew you could learn so much about brave parenting from a duck or some tropical fish?

Releasing Our Agenda

Deuteronomy 6:5-7 says,

> Love the Lord your God with all your heart and with all your soul and with all your strength. These commandments that I give you today are to be upon your hearts. Impress them on your children. Talk about them when you sit at home and when you walk along the road, when you lie down and when you get up.

Oh, how I felt so convicted one day when I heard a sermon on this. I had been focusing on teaching my children how to read, dress themselves, and write their letters, as well as working on their speech, gross and fine motor skills. Sure, we'd pray before bedtime and meals, but why read Bible stories I wasn't even sure they could grasp when there were so many things they needed to learn? I figured they were learning about Jesus at church and so I could focus on the other stuff, the academic and life skills stuff. Then when they were older, maybe we could learn about Jesus.

So I put off reading Bible stories and instead read their favorite books. I put off teaching them Scripture and instead taught them how to say they wanted to eat.

But *Matthew 19:13-15* says

> Then little children were brought to Jesus for him to place his hands on them and pray for them. But the disciples rebuked those who brought them.
> Jesus said, 'Let the little children come to me, and do not hinder them, for the kingdom of heaven belongs to such as these.'

Ouch again. I felt so convicted that I was hindering my children from knowing about Jesus and their Bible stories because I thought they were too delayed to get it yet. But worse yet, I had become convinced there were lessons that were more important and urgent that my children needed to learn now—lessons that were more essential than learning about God and salvation.

Since then we have gotten more intentional about praying together as a family. About reading Bible stories before bed. About listening to children's praise songs and singing them together. And when my oldest son uttered his first prayer before dinner, though my husband and I understood only a word or two that he said, our hearts were overjoyed. God knew what that child prayed for.

And when one night before bed I asked my son what he was thankful for and he responded "Eesus!" it brought tears to my eyes and hope to my heart. My son may not be able to say his J's, but he knows about Jesus, and that the most important thing I could ever teach him.

We have been commanded to teach our children about Jesus. Even if it takes decades before they can grasp and accept salvation, or maybe it is something they may never fully grasp, we need to keep teaching them, because it's what we've been commanded to do.

A quick note for those mamas whose children may be nonverbal or cognitively disabled and you are worried they may never be able to accept Christ and experience salvation. First of all, God is very loving and merciful, "The Lord is good to everyone. He showers compassion on all of his creation" (*Psalm 145:9*). He will not forsake the child He lovingly and uniquely created.

Also, He knows what is in the hearts and minds of our children, which is a lot more than we may ever realize.

> And [Jesus] said, "Truly I tell you, unless you change and become like little children, you will never enter the kingdom of heaven. Therefore, whoever takes the lowly position of this child is the greatest in the kingdom of heaven" (Matthew 18:3-5).

Your child, whether an adult or a young child has an innocent faith like the little children He loved so dearly and invited to come to Him. He used them as the example of what true faith is like and tells us that they are welcome in the kingdom of heaven.

Reflection Questions

1. Have you been more like Mary or Martha in caring for your children?
2. What things have you been trying to control?
3. Have you ever released your children into God's care? How did you feel afterward?
4. Do you struggle with letting your child try new things? If so, why?
5. What are a few self-help skills, chores, etc. you could let your child do on his/her own?

6. What actions can you take to be more intentional about teaching your children about God?

Chapter 7

Embracing Your Husband

Different studies spout different statistics of the higher divorce rate for couples raising children with special needs. Marriage is hard enough. Add in some children, especially ones who have more needs than typical children, and it makes marriage that much harder. It becomes easy to put the kids first, to have different ideas how about the kids should be cared for, and to have different ways of grieving your child's diagnosis and challenges.

I encourage you to guard your heart against this high statistic. Marriage is precious and sacred to God and needs to be protected. Claim victory in your marriage, that you will be fully committed to your marriage vows.

This chapter is challenging to write because each marriage is personal and different for every couple, and yet it is so very precious to God and so it must be included in this book. You may be unmarried, divorced, separated, or really struggling in your marriage. What I share in this chapter is straight from God's word, and not meant to make you feel guilty, for "there is therefore now no condemnation for those who are in Christ Jesus" (*Romans 8:1*). If you are feeling guilt or condemnation, that is not from God and is something you must release, so that you can embrace how God intends our marriages to be.

I have experienced a lot of struggles in my own marriage, and have also experienced so much victory in my marriage, and I want you to experience that too.

Why We Often Want More from Our Husbands

I love my husband dearly. But like most couples, we are opposites in many ways. He loves structure, organization, and productivity. My motto is "I put the pro in procrastination." I'm totally content with a pile of clothes on the floor or a pile of bills and other papers on the kitchen counter. Both of those piles will be dealt with. Eventually. And I know which pile contains which item. Most of the time.

My desire is to love on and teach my children. The dishes and laundry can wait. I also am committed to writing and blogging, a task I firmly believe God has called me to. Writing, social media, and blogging can take up time that I could be taking care of things around the house.

On the other hand, my husband was taught to do everything to the best and utmost of his ability . Less than perfection demonstrates you don't care. So when we got married and my husband found ways I could be trying harder around the house, he didn't hesitate to tell me so. But it hurt deeply every time he found something I could be doing better. Whether it was a more efficient way of loading the dishwasher, or how to organize our mail, what I heard from him was you're doing it wrong and you're not good enough.

It made me angry. Defensive. I wanted to hear he was proud of me. That I was good enough for him.

No matter how much we argued or discussed this issue, neither of us changed. I knew what I wanted from my husband, and because he couldn't give me what I wanted, I thought he was messed up. Or that I was messed up. But no matter how much I wanted my husband to be more laid back and more encouraging and less questioning of the way I did things, it simply is not how God made him.

Why do we have so much contention with our husbands? Why is so hard to love them all the time? One, because our flesh is sinful and prideful and we are always fighting with our flesh. But the second reason is found in *Genesis 2:16*. Because of the fall, because of sin in our life, we not only are cursed with painful childbirth, but "your desire will be for your husband, and he will rule over you."

It means that we will always be wanting more of them and more from them. That we want them to support us more emotionally. To be more like us or more like we envision a good husband to be. To be the fathers to our children that we want them to be. And on and on it goes, if we let it. But that causes us to feel bitter and disappointed. To voice our anger and nag our husbands. To make them feel like they are not providing enough for their families.

Embracing Our Husband's God Given Roles

All the way back in *Genesis 2:15*, "The LORD God took the man and put him in the Garden of Eden to work it and protect it."

There are two jobs that God bestowed upon the man: to work for and to protect his home and family.

God designed your husband to provide for his family. Yes, sometimes our lives demand that both husband and wife work. Or if there is no husband in the picture, the woman must work to provide for her family. But if your husband is fulfilling his role of providing for his family, of bringing home a paycheck that pays your bills, puts food on the table, and pays for all those therapies, well then he is fulfilling his role as the provider.

And the second role *Genesis 2:15* says the man is to protect his home. A husband fulfilling this role will have different ways of doing that. He may have ideas about how the budget should be spent so the family will be protected financially and no one will go hungry. He may have a particular way he wants something cared for in the home so he knows his family is living in a safe and clean home.

After years of contention with my husband, lots of tears and arguments and prayers, one day, God helped me see that my husband is a visionary. My husband sees the big picture and he sees the details. He sees how to make things better. Those are all characteristics of God. And once I saw my husband in that way, it was marriage transforming. Whenever my husband questions why things were done a certain way, I naturally get defensive. But I'm training myself to remember this is the way God made my husband. God made him to take care of his family, to protect his family, and this is how he does it. It may not be the way I want him to, but he is doing exactly what God made him do, and I need to embrace it. Not just embrace it, but appreciate my husband's desire to fight for his family by ensuring things are done a certain way.

I must include one disclaimer here before we move on. God made the husband to provide for and protect your family. If your husband is not fulfilling his role as protector and instead harming you or your children in any way intentionally, whether that be physically or emotionally, that is another story. He is sinning and you have been forced to step into the role of primary protector. In this case, you MUST get outside help. God does not want any of his children to be hurt—that includes you and your children.

Embracing Our Role as Helper

So to recap, it's the husband's job to provide for and protect the home and the family. Because of sin, the men were cursed with hard work and painful toil (*Genesis 2:17-19*). No longer do they work in the peaceful garden, they work out in the wild, where the work is hard and often unappreciated, where the stress is high and there is sin and struggle.

And when our husbands come home, they are tired and want the home to be a place that is less stressful than work. To be a sanctuary after the wildness of their workplace.

Wives, that's where we come in. In *Genesis 2:16* "The LORD God said, 'It is not good for the man to be alone. I will make a helper suitable for him.'"

These men we married, our princes, our knights in shining armor, were not created to simply meet all our needs. Nope, they have quite a few of their own, and it is our role to help them. They go to work and they come home tired. They need our encouragement. They need us to pray over them. To make the house a safe place for them to come home to. They want to feel needed and respected and that we genuinely care about them and their needs.

Our role is also stated in *Titus 2:4-5*, "Wives are to love their husbands and children, to be self-controlled and pure, to be busy at home, to be kind, and to be subject to their husbands."

For most women, it comes naturally to us to love our children and be busy at home. But the other areas do not come as naturally. Especially the love their husbands, be kind, be subject to their husbands bit. Our husbands are grown men and can take of themselves, right? Our children need us, and they have a lot of needs. And we forget, our husbands have needs that we were created to fulfill.

Proverbs 31:10-12 says "A wife of noble character who can find? She is worth far more than rubies. Her husband has full confidence in her and lacks nothing of value. She brings him good, not harm, all the days of her life."

We have a lot of power as wives to help our husbands grow more into the man God created him to be. Not by manipulating or nagging him, but rather by encouraging him and letting him know that you are care for him at home, while he is working to provide for your family. We have the power to make our homes a sanctuary our husbands are eager to come home to after a hard day at work.

Think about the little things and the big things you could do to show him you care and are fighting for him too. Maybe when he comes home from work, instead of complaining how hard of a day you've had or how much you need him to help you, or you keep doing what you're doing and barely acknowledge he is home, you take a moment to give him a kiss or a hug and ask how his day went and tell him you're really glad he's home. Encourage him with the things you appreciate about him and watch him stand just a tiny bit taller. Do the task your husband asked you

to do but you've been avoiding doing. Take time after the kids
are in bed to talk about your marriage, your heart, his heart, and
what you could be doing for each other to show each other you
care. Reminisce about the good times. Hold hands. Embrace
your husband physically, emotionally, and spiritually. Pray together. Give him an opportunity to pursue a hobby or passion
he hasn't had a lot of time for lately. Give him a gift just because
you love him. Pray over him before he goes to work. Read a book
about marriage together, such as *Love and Respect*, or *The Five
Love Languages for Couples*. Find a babysitter (easier said than
done, right, but oh so important) and go on a date, or to a marriage conference, or if you need to, to marriage counseling. Can't
find a babysitter? Some of our favorite memories are when one
of us would go pick up dinner and we'd have a picnic dinner in
the living room after the kids were in bed and just chat. Now that
the kids are in school, my husband and I try to meet up for lunch
at least twice a month. Be creative and think of a few ways you
could show your husband you care.

When your life revolves around caring for your kids the thought
of doing more things for your hubby and your marriage seems
daunting. You believe your husband is able to take care of himself and your children cannot. But that's not the truth. Our husbands desperately need us, even if they won't admit it. It's the
way God made us. He said "It's not good for man to be alone."
Don't think just cooking meals and doing the laundry shows your
husband you care. He may appreciate your hard work, but it
doesn't show you care about him as an individual, as your soul-
mate and friend.

You made a commitment to love, honor, and cherish your husband. In the good times and bad. In sickness and in health—though you didn't know it when you made that vow, that vow would include your children. Let him know you love, honor, and cherish him.

Embracing the Special Needs Journey Together

Speaking of the vow in sickness and in health: You and your husband may have different ways of dealing with your child's special needs. He may not go to the appointments. He may not want to talk about your child's needs. He may not seem as invested as you are in the therapies and the research that you are doing. Or he may have lots of ideas about what to do and go to the appointments with you or take turns going to the appointments. He is dealing with this journey differently than you.

But that doesn't mean he's not experiencing his own grief and all that other stuff we've been dealing with in this book. Embrace that he is dealing with the journey differently than you are, but determine to embrace each other as you travel this journey.

Share how both of you are really feeling about your child's challenges and diagnosis. Talk through your worries, your fears, your unmet expectations about what parenthood would be like. Share in the grief together.

And recognize the grief may come in cycles. You both may be in a good place, and then something will happen that will set one of you or both of you back into a pit of grief and worry. Support each other in the good times and the bad.

I shared in the last chapter how I needed to release control of my children. One of the ways I did that was to invite my husband in to help me. We had to work together to determine what was best for our children because we both had different ideas, but once we merged them together we were able to create a plan that fit our budget and gave us more time together as a family. We evaluated every therapy we were doing and stuck with those that were helping the most. We decided to take breaks from therapy on occasion, so we could have time to rest, to be a family, to go on vacation, and simply to let our kids be kids. (Repeat after me, it's ok to take a break from therapy once in a while!)

Invite your husband into the process, ask for his opinion, and respect what he has to offer. Support each other's weaknesses, celebrate each other's strengths, and work as a team to do what is best for your whole family.

Though both Naomi and Ruth were dealing with grief, Ruth determined to stay with her mother-in-law and face their challenging circumstances together, as a committed team. She said to her mother-in-law what many of us say in our marriage vows:

> Don't urge me to leave you or to turn back from you. Where you go I will go, and where you stay I will stay. Your people will be my people and your God my God. Where you die I will die, and there I will be buried (Ruth 2:18)

Determine to be like Ruth, fully committed to your partner as you travel the special needs parenting journey together.

Reflection Questions

1. What is your marriage like now? In what areas would you like it to be different?
2. What do the majority of your arguments reveal about your husband's view of providing for and protecting his family?
3. How could seeing your husband's qualities as ways that God uniquely made him change your marriage?
4. How could you show your husband more love, respect, and appreciation?
5. How could you and your husband be better teammates in this special needs journey together?

Chapter 8

Releasing Insecurity

One Wednesday in March a few years ago, I took my boys to their occupational and speech therapy appointments. We'd been wearing long sleeved shirts and jackets everywhere we went. By the time we made it to our appointment, it was getting quite warm. After unbuckling the kiddos from their car seats, I took off their jackets, grabbed all the necessities we needed while we were there for their appointments, and we went inside.

The first detail I noticed: everyone was wearing t-shirts. Some were even wearing shorts. And a lot of the kids in the waiting room were in sandals. I looked over at my boys, who moments ago were wearing jackets and were now clad in their long sleeved shirts, jeans, socks, and sneakers.

I started playing the "should have" game. *I should have checked the weather. I should have pulled out their summer clothes by now.* I could go on and on, but I'll spare you the details, because

I'm sure you've played the "should have" game too, or something similar. I had an entire hour to allow my thoughts to spiral out of control, and by the end of the appointment, I was convinced I was the worst mother in the world.

But then my older son walked over to me after his appointment. He had a grin on his face and I'll never forget the words he said. The words were unintelligible to the other moms waiting in that room with me, but I got the message loud and clear.

"You gold star Mommy." On the end of my child's finger was a gold star sticker which he placed on my shirt. Tears filled my eyes and I gave that precious child a hug, thankful for the encouragement and truth that I desperately needed.

I didn't feel like a gold star mommy, but I was basing that on my own thoughts and feelings and high expectations. My child told me I was a gold star mommy and he genuinely meant it.

I was looking through my own eyes and seeing only my shortcomings, and not looking through the eyes of the ones that matter. The ones that love me unconditionally. Not just my children but God Himself, who created me and delights over me (*Zephaniah 3:16*).

After that appointment, I placed that gold star sticker on a picture of my children above my desk. It is a gentle reminder that regardless of how I may feel about myself, I am loved by the ones that matter the most to me.

Releasing the Lies

Renee Swope, who also happens to be a special needs mama, wrote in one of my favorite books, *A Confident Heart*, something that has changed my life and the way I try to think about myself. She says:

> In the same way a radio has AM and FM frequencies, so do our thoughts. They are either AM (Against Me) or FM (For Me) thoughts. Many times we can be our worst critics, and we have a lot of AM thoughts. We also have an enemy who is completely against us. He is jealous of God's glory in us and threatened by the beauty that lies within the heart of a woman whose identity is secure. That is why he attacks our confidence. He knows if he can paralyze us with self-doubt and insecurity we will never live up to the full potential of who we are and what we have in Christ ... Our enemy knows if he can influence the way we think, then our thoughts will determine how we feel, and our feelings will shape how we live. But we're not going to let that happen anymore. [5] [6]

Recognizing that you're having an AM thought and immediately exchanging it for a FM thought does wonders for our minds, our souls, and our identities.

Renee Swope says that when Satan "can paralyze us with self-doubt and insecurity, we will never live up to the potential of who we are and what we have in Christ." How cruel of Satan to attack our very identity.

Now, when I find myself starting to play the "should have" game, or the "I'm not ___ enough" game, I remember *Philippians 4:8*, "Finally brothers, whatever is true, whatever is noble, whatever is right, whatever is pure, whatever is lovely, whatever is admirable–if anything is excellent or praiseworthy–think about such things."

As soon as I catch myself playing the "should have" game, I immediately put *Philippians 4:8* into practice. Just because I made a mistake does not mean I am a bad mom. If God can give me grace (unmerited favor, or basically a whole lot of forgiveness) for all my sin, surely I can give myself grace for making one mistake.

Oh, just imagine how different your life would be if you didn't believe the lies and insecurities, but instead believed God's truths!

It's important to tell yourself God's truth. That you are a good mom. That you're doing a great job. That you are beautiful and gifted and God has a purpose for your life. It's important to forgive yourself when you make a mistake and not dwell on it. It's time we show ourselves the same kindness and grace God shows us.

Releasing Guilt

In moms groups and in special needs moms groups, there is one thing I always find–mother's guilt. Mothers asking questions about how often others do something, to see if they measure up. Mothers asking to see if others did something in particular when they were pregnant or when their kids were babies, to see if maybe they were responsible for something. Mothers asking how often you do a certain therapy to see if they should be doing more. There's a constant worry that we're not doing enough, or we did something wrong, or we should be doing things differently and we're not afraid to let others know of our worries. We joke about having mother's guilt as if it is a badge of honor, a sign we are good mothers caring so much for our children. But that's not how God wants us to live.

Mother's guilt shows up in the Bible too. But in this case, it's not a mother coming up to Jesus asking if she's guilty, but society trying to determine if indeed she is guilty.

> As [Jesus] went along, he saw a man blind from birth. His disciples asked him, 'Rabbi, who sinned, this man or his parents, that he was born blind?'
> 'Neither this man nor his parents sinned,' said Jesus, 'but this happened so that the work of God might be displayed in his life'. (John 9:1-3)

Jesus freed the blind man and the parents from wondering if maybe it was something they did that caused this man's blindness. And then if that wasn't relief enough, He gave sight to this man.

I don't know God's purpose for our child's diagnosis, but I do know that somehow it brings God glory. It could be to teach us new things, opening our eyes to a whole new world we were unaware of before. Or to humble us and make us rely on Him like never before. To provide awesome testimonies. To bring healing to our children, either in their lifetime or in heaven. To help us encourage others going through similar struggles. To encourage those around us with our faith and trust in God despite our circumstances. But regardless, it is for His glory. His kingdom is being revealed in our children.

But constantly feeling this mother's guilt is not of God. He looks at us and He doesn't see our sins and our guilt like we do. *Psalm 103:12* says "As far as the east is from the west, so far has he removed our transgressions from us." He sees the beautiful, gifted you He created, not all your sin and shame.

Jesus says, "No one who puts his hand to the plow and looks back is fit for the service in the kingdom of God" (*Luke 9:62*). These were words Jesus told a man wanting to go back to his family and say goodbye before he followed Jesus. But Jesus is telling this man he can't keep looking back to how things were in the past. You'll notice many of the things you feel guilty about happened in the past, which we cannot change anyway. Constantly looking behind you while plowing means you're going to have lots of uneven rows. You're not focused on where you're going. You're stuck in the past and unable to enjoy the present. Unable to move into the future without fear.

Sometimes our guilt can be about the present and how we want it to be different to create a better future. We do have control over our present moment, and we can choose what we do with it. For example, I started feeling guilty that I was spending more time online than I was with my children when we are home together. And so I made it my goal to play with the kids before I go online, to limit the amount of time I spent online. In that case, it's not guilt but a conviction from God about how to make things better. If you feel convicted about something you can change, then please do make the change. But we must let go of guilt about things in the past.

Jesus died so we would be free from all guilt. Jesus died to give us the freedom to be victorious women. Women who are wonderful, loving mothers who make so many sacrifices for their children. And Satan has lied to us, telling us we are not doing enough as women and mothers, we should have done more or be doing more now. This is not how Jesus wants us to live.

How do we let go of guilt? We accept the truth that God says we are righteous, we are His daughters, we are reconciled to Him, we are created to do good works, we are created to be blessings to our families. If we live in our identity, live how God sees us, the guilt will melt away.

Releasing Negative Thinking

I once watched a French Dove commercial titled "Inner Critic" in which women were asked to write in a journal every negative thought they had about themselves for a day. Later on, they gave two actresses scripts with the lines these women had written down. Both actresses read over the scripts astounded, saying

"I have to say that? But it's horrible!"

The actresses dutifully memorized their lines and said them aloud to each other in a coffee shop, where all the unsuspecting journal-writing women were sitting, as well as a few other people.

Everyone in the cafe was appalled to hear the things the two actresses were saying. One of the women finally stood up and told the actresses to stop because what they were saying was "harsh" and "violent."

The journal writers confessed how horrifying it was to hear the things they said to themselves aloud, but even more so, said to other people. They realized the good qualities they did have but weren't focusing on. The Dove commercial ends with a question "When was the last beautiful thought you had about yourself?"

We say things to ourselves we would never say to another human being, and then we wonder why we feel lost, stuck, not good enough, etc. We doubt that God can love us. All that negative thinking is not from God and is not good for us at all–spiritually, mentally, or even physically.

About a year ago I listened to a TedX Talk called "Ridiculous" by Dr. Caroline Leaf. She is a Christian neurobiologist who states that toxic thoughts can have a toxic effect on your brain and body, and positive thinking can have positive effects on the brain and the body. She says God made it that way, and that's why there's so much Scripture on fixing our minds on God and on positive things. That if we are trusting in Him, trusting in His truths, then our bodies, our hearts, minds, our entire lives will be blessed.

God has a beautiful recipe for us to experience more of the abundant life He came to give us, and it comes in the way of thinking positively. "Do not conform yourselves anymore to the pattern of this world, but be transformed by the renewing of your mind" (*Romans 12:2*).

Remember at the end of that Dove commercial, when they asked "When was the last beautiful thought you had about yourself?" Feel free to answer it. But then ask, "What was the last beautiful thought God had about you?" God has more beautiful thoughts about you than you will ever know in your lifetime.

When a negative thought pops into your head, you have the power to renew your mind, to banish that negative thought and focus on God's beautiful thoughts about you. That you are a beloved child of God. That you are fearfully and wonderfully made. That God gives you the strength to do all things. That you are chosen, forgiven and redeemed. That He delights in you and rejoices over you with singing. That He has created you to do good things. That He has a plan and a purpose for you and your children.

And on and on the beautiful thoughts go.

Reflection Questions

1. Is the majority of your guilt about things you can change, or cannot change? What must you do with those things you feel guilty about?

2. What is the biggest lie you tell yourself?

3. What is the biggest lie you believe about yourself as a mother?

4. How would your life be different if you didn't believe the lies and insecurities and instead believed God's truths about you?

5. What beautiful thoughts does God think about you?

Chapter 9

Embracing You

One thing I've noticed about the mom journey in general, but especially the special needs mom journey, is that it's easy to neglect yourself. It's easy to put your children and their needs ahead of your own. It's easy to put taking care of the house and running the errands and putting food on the table ahead of yourself. To live in survival mode rather than in thriving mode.

It feels selfish to do what I want to do when there are so many things to do and my children need so much of me. It may feel counter-intuitive to plan how to do more of what makes us feel good instead of doing more for our families. But, more than likely your husband, your children, and the people around you want to see you happy. A happy mom makes a happy home. And if you take time to refill your cup, then you have more good things to pour out to others.

Embracing Your Health

It is easy for us to put our children's needs ahead of our own. We run ourselves ragged, our stress levels are sky high, and our health suffers. There is a report that says that special needs parents experience similar levels of stress to that of soldiers in combat. Our bodies were not meant to handle that much stress for such long periods of time. Exhaustion and health problems will follow.

Paul tells us,

> Do you not know that your body is a temple of the Holy Spirit, who is in you, whom you have received from God? You are not your own. You were bought at a price. Therefore, honor God with your body (1 Corinthians 6:19-20).

It is so easy to think that our health affects only us. But how you treat your body shows God how much you respect the body He has given you. And the healthier our bodies, the more energy we have to love and serve the people who are important to us and to the kingdom of God.

After my younger son was born, I was caring for a newborn and a toddler with an endless schedule of appointments. I started having lots of problems with my own health. My digestion was terrible, and my stomach was so bloated people assumed I was expecting again. Anxiety and depression hit. I had pain in my joints, and my face broke out in acne worse than when I was a teenager. I struggled with insomnia and was exhausted all day long. I craved sugar every moment of the day. But I ignored all the health problems, drank lots of coffee to keep me going, and gave in to my sugar cravings, consuming an unhealthy amount of chocolate throughout my day. I had to focus on my children. And I put myself on the back burner. Until, finally, I couldn't take it any longer. I was an exhausted, uncomfortable mess.

So, I started eating healthier and drastically reduced my sugar intake. I drank more water. I started going for daily walks with the kiddos in a stroller. Slowly, I felt better. Although it wasn't easy and I missed some of my favorite foods, I did not miss the way they made me feel. I was glad to be doing what was best for my body, the one that God created just for me, and slowly but steadily I regained my health.

Oh, and don't forget about rest! Throughout both the Old and the New Testaments we are commanded and encouraged to rest. In addition to that, we see that God Himself rested on the seventh day, modeling for us what He wants us to do.

Jesus was a busy man. People were constantly coming up to Him, asking Him questions, and begging for healing. He would stop and talk to them, touch them, love them, and heal them. He had to wake up early in the morning just to get some alone time with God, when people wouldn't be all around him. He had parables to tell, a kingdom to preach, and people to heal. And in the end, He had to bring salvation to the world. But Jesus also rested, sneaking moments early in the morning or in between sermons and healing people to rest and to pray. In *Mark 6:31-32* He even encouraged His disciples to join Him and rest.

Yes, Jesus was busy. But He was busy doing exactly what God asked of Him. And He took opportunities to rest and spend time with the His Father. If the God of the universe needed a day to rest after creating the world, if Jesus needed to rest and to spend time with God daily, how much more do we need rest? How much more do we need to know God's plan for us, so we are busy doing the things God wants us to be busy doing?

And speaking of rest, sometimes it's good for everyone in your family to take a break from all the therapies and appointments and just spend time together. Go on vacation. Or just have a week off to relax and be a family together. I know for a long time I was adamant about not missing a single appointment, but once we started taking therapy breaks from time to time, I actually noticed a boost in progress. It's like having a chance for your kids to rest gives their brains and bodies a chance to integrate all they've been learning. And everyone in your family will enjoy taking time to slow down and just enjoy the good things in life.

Embracing Your Gifts and Passions

Sometimes, I view the *Proverbs 31* woman as an intimidating woman. She did it all, and with a smile on her face. But one time, I read it with her gifts and passions in mind. She obviously loved her family and taking care of them. She also liked to care for her vineyard. To help the people in her community in need.

And she liked to sew. Seriously, verse after verse talks about her sewing. I hated that because I detest sewing. If a button pops off, I'll procrastinate for months on sewing that thing back on.

My lack of sewing skills and organization made me feel far short of the *Proverbs 31* woman. But Scripture indicates she found joy in making clothes for her family and covers for their beds. If she didn't, she would have had her servants sew and garden for her, right? Yes, ladies, she had servants! She didn't do everything herself! Another reassuring realization that I'm not as far off from being the *Proverbs 31* woman I originally thought. She made time for the garden and the sewing, not because she had to, but because she wanted to. And her family found joy in it and viewed her as blessed.

God made us with gifts and passions and dreams. Now, don't get me wrong, there are seasons of life where we may have to put some of our dreams and passions on hold. Caring for children, especially ones with extra needs, is definitely a busy season. But even in that busy season, God doesn't want us to lose ourselves and how He created us.

God is a creative being. He made the world, He made us. He made us to create too. In *Exodus 31:1-6* God tells Moses about how He designed and gifted Bezalei to be the one to build the tabernacle. God says

> I have filled him with the Spirit of God, with skill, ability and knowledge in all kinds of crafts-to make artistic designs for work in gold, silver and bronze, to cut and set stones, to work in wood, and to engage in all kinds of craftsmanship.

First of all, I find it amazing that this is the first time in Scripture where a person is said to be filled with the Spirit of God. Sure, prophets and other mighty men and women of God were filled with the Spirit, but the first person in Scripture reported as being filled with the Spirit isn't Noah, Abraham, or Moses, but Bezalei, the man set apart to design the tabernacle. There is power in whatever passion or gift you have been given.

Secondly, you can sense the pride in God's voice as He brags about Bezalei and how he is using his gifts and skills. And it makes the parable of the talents in *Matthew 25:14-30* all the more real. The manager gave three of his servants talents of silver. The first two servants did something with the talents they were given. And the manager was proud of them and blessed them with even more talents and gifts. But the third servant did nothing with his. He simply buried it in the ground. And the manager was furious with him. Translation: God wants us to use the gifts, talents, and passions He has given us.

Being a special needs mom is not an excuse for not stewarding your gifts and talents. It's understandable when you're exhausted and busy to not have the time or energy to pursue your gifts and talents. But there is a reason you feel alive and renewed when you do something you love to do and have been gifted to do.

It's because you were born to do it, regardless of how busy your life is.

All of us have a desire in our hearts to create something. Maybe it's writing a blog. Maybe it's quilting, knitting, painting, cooking good food, or making beautiful music. Maybe it's connecting with other women and leading a small group or a children's ministry at church or working for a non-profit. Maybe it's your own business. You know what it is. You can feel it in your heart. It's time to let go of that mom guilt we may feel when pursuing something that interests us, because God created us to be more than just mothers and wives. He bestowed gifts and passions on us, and He wants us to use them for His glory and for our joy.

Keep taking care of yourself and using your gifts and passions. Keep on being you, the you God created you to be, and everyone close to you will be blessed.

Reflection Questions

1. Is self-care a priority in your life?
2. What would you like to do to take better care of your health?
3. What can you do to ensure you get proper rest?
4. What are your dreams and passions? How could you make more time for them in your life?
5. Make some time to reflect on your day-to-day schedule, your weekly calendar, etc. Make a list of the things you do each day and how much you spend doing it. How much

of what you do is for God? For your children? For your husband? For yourself?

Chapter 10

Embracing Community

There have been a lot of surprises about this special needs journey. The one I find the most surprising, and honestly the most devastating to my soul, is the loneliness and isolation.

Before being a special needs mama I was a social butterfly, involved in lots of groups, leading Bible studies, chatting with coworkers and strangers alike. I loved being around people.

But when my sons' delays began and the differences between them and their peers got more noticeable, my social life got harder. Lonelier.

In the span of five years we had moved three times, so three different times we had to start over, meeting new people, finding new therapists, and making friends at a new church. When is it appropriate to share with these new people how much you are really struggling?

I struggled with how much I should share about our challenges with anybody. How much to tell my family? How much to tell my friends, who now lived on the other side of the country? How much do I tell these new people I am meeting? How much do I share on Facebook and Instagram?

At that time, the people I felt closest to were my childrens' teachers and therapists.

I put on a cheerful smile that painted a happy, cheerful life and a deep love for God that was far from how I was living. And I suffered alone, with only my husband to offer me the support I really needed from having a good friend or two in my life.

When times are tough, we tend to want to be alone, or we fear reaching out to others, but that's when we need each other the most. God made us to need each other, to support each other.

From God creating Eve because it wasn't good for Adam to be alone, to prophets and other biblical characters being blessed with companions, to the creation of the church who met to encourage each other, fellowship, serve, and praise God together (*Acts 2:42-47*), it's obvious God wants us to be in community.

We are not meant to travel life alone. And yet in our fast-paced culture, that's what happens to a lot of us. Our connections are plentiful online, but our real life connections are few and far between. We are starving for connection, for companionship, for a friend and a community to help us in our time of need.

Embracing Community for Yourself

There's a passage I read one day that totally changed my perspective on how I'd been living. It's found in *2 Kings 7:3-9*, situated in the middle of a great famine in the city of Samaria. The Arameans had surrounded the city, cutting off all their access to supplies so that they experienced a great famine until they surrendered.

It is in these trying circumstances we meet four men who learn how to be a community.

> Now there were four men with leprosy at the entrance of the city gate. They said to each other, 'Why stay here until we die? If we say, "We'll go into the city" the famine is there and we will die. And if we stay here, we will die. So let's go over the camp of the Arameans and surrender. If they spare us, we live. If they kill us, then we die' (2 Kings 7:3-4).

These four men were all experiencing a similar trial. They all had been shunned by their culture because of their disease. They could relate to the physical, emotional, and spiritual pain the others were experiencing and had established a friendship of sorts. I don't know if they became fast friends doing everything together, or if they just happened to meet at the gate at certain times of the day and share in their misery together, or if maybe this day they met each other for the very first time.

Regardless, they were not alone. They had found each other for support. And because they had support, because they were not alone anymore, they had the courage to do something. To not just sit at the gate and complain about their circumstances until they died, but to do something that could change their lives and the lives of others as well. You can read the full story in *2 Kings 7:5-9*, but basically the lepers go to the Aramean camp. And God shows up, making the Arameans believe the lepers are an entire army of chariots and horses and so they run away in fear. And the lepers go into the camp and find a feast. They take their fill and collect up silver and gold and other treasures. And then, they decide they shouldn't keep these treasures to themselves, that they'll share it with others who are also suffering because of the famine.

Look at all the wealth, the blessings that these men suddenly experienced. God paved the way for them to experience a banquet after all the hunger and desperation they had been experiencing. God wants us to experience that too! He doesn't want us to sit alone, feeling miserable about our circumstances and feeling utterly alone.

> Two are better than one,
> because they have a good return for their work;
> If one falls down,
> His friend can help him up.
> But pity the man who falls
> And has no one to help him up!
> Also, if two lie down together, they will keep warm,
> But how can one keep warm alone?
> Though one may be overpowered,

Two can defend themselves.

A cord of three strands is not quickly broken (Ecclesiastes 4:9-12).

I remember I was desperate for a best friend right after we'd moved and we'd started getting diagnosis after diagnosis. Sure, I had my friends from before, we'd email on occasion, schedule occasional phone dates, stay in touch through Facebook, but it wasn't the same.

So I prayed for a friend. And then I decided to make my prayer specific. I prayed for a friend whose child also had special needs, someone who could relate to my journey and share it with me, like those lepers at the gate.

It didn't happen immediately, but God answered. And the way He answered was way beyond what I could have imagined.

One day, I was going to a moms' meet-up group. I'd had a few good playdates with this group but was contemplating this one being my last because playdates can be hard. And that morning, everything in me wanted to just stay home and rest on our one appointment-free day. But something inside of me whispered I should go. So there I was at the playdate, watching my older son play with the other kids while my younger son contentedly napped in his stroller. My attention was suddenly drawn to a child I hadn't seen at the playdates before, a child not much older than my son. I was mesmerized by this child who seemed so much like my son. And all of a sudden I just knew this child had the same apraxia diagnosis as my son, and so as soon as his mother was done with her conversation with another mother I practically ran over to her and asked her if her son was talking yet.

She looked at me funny, and I understood why. It's a weird question to ask someone you'd never met before. One that no one has dared to ask me before. But she answered honestly. And she told me exactly what I suspected: her little guy had apraxia too.

We talked for a long time, and scheduled another play date for just the two of us and our children. And decided to start ourselves a support group because we both needed a friend and needed support desperately. We both felt God answered a deep cry of our hearts that day. The support group we created lasted only about a year before she moved and then I moved. And though we advertised about the group, we were the only two members in our support group the entire time. But it was a great year. A year when I felt hope again. When I had a friend who could relate to my journey. A friendship where we could exchange ideas and concerns and victories and laughs.

She and I were like the lepers at the gate. We shared in the journey together, even if it was only for a year. And we were eager to share our new joy with others. We didn't want to keep it to ourselves and so we started a local support group for parents of children with apraxia.

This doesn't mean we can share our heart with everyone. Unfortunately, not everyone in our lives is supportive, encouraging, or understanding of our situation. I've definitely been hurt by comments friends and family members have said, whether their comments were meant to be hurtful or not. But you still need people. You need to find yourself a tribe of people you can trust. Supportive family members and friends. A support group in your area. A small group at your church. A Christian counselor. And experience blessing by doing so.

We are not meant to sit alone at a gate, feeling lost and alone and purposeless. We are made for action. We are made for relationships. We are made to share our stories. The lepers realized this and experienced blessing not only for themselves, but their city. They didn't get the instant healing they probably longed for, but God provided for them in ways they couldn't have predicted and a companionship that probably spanned the remainder of their lives.

Take off that mask and let people see what's going on in your heart. Not on social media, but with a person who will listen to your heart and love you regardless. Let people see what God is teaching you. Let people see the good, the bad, and the beautiful that is you.

Embracing Community for Your Children

Have I mentioned before how hard playdates were for me? Well, so were a lot of community events—events that sounded like fun but would not be fun for my family.

Being out in the community led to the biggest struggles for me.

Comparing my children to others. Watching my younger son get overstimulated and either have a meltdown or become aggressive with other children. Watching my older son get picked on by others or called "baby" because he wasn't talking yet. Knowing places we went wouldn't have the accommodations my children needed or the food they could eat.

It became easy to isolate ourselves, to stay home, away from watchful eyes, meltdown triggers, and lack of accommodations. But I realized this was doing me and my children no favors. I was lonely, and my children were not growing in their social skills or their awareness of the world by being home with me all day.

So I started being intentional about getting my boys out into environments that would be safe for them. I would set up a playdate with a close friend and her kids, instead of attending a mom's meetup with lots of people. I enrolled my children in a school where they could learn and interact with others. I enrolled them in a swimming lesson class and a My Gym class specifically for children with special needs (yep, they exist!). I would drop them off at children's church or at Vacation Bible School at a church I trusted.

It is our job to train up our children in the way they should go (*Proverbs 22:6*), and learning to interact with others is an area of training for my boys—to learn how to share and show kindness and to learn how to communicate with others, whether it's through verbal speech, sign language, or a communication device.

They also need to learn about the world around them. It's easy to want to shelter them from it. From the stares, the hurtful comments, and the challenges that come from the fallen world we live in. Our children unfortunately may learn more about the hardness of life than their peers, but they will grow stronger from it. They will persevere in ways that children who have it easy will never experience.

My children have learned so much by going out into the world around them. Lessons about nature, people, and other cultures, how to buy items from the store, how to interact with animals and with people, how to build a sandcastle. It's hard. I get it. But our children need opportunities to grow with their peers and people of all ages and types. And our children, whether they realize it or not, have the opportunity to teach others about life. That is something I don't want to hide from the world.

It may be corny, but I think of my children when I hear the song "This Little Light of Mine." My children are the light of my life. I don't want to hide my children under a bushel. I definitely don't want Satan (or the world) to blow them out. I want my children to shine brightly, to show the world their own uniqueness, and for them to bring God glory. It takes courage to let them shine. Our protective instinct is to keep them safe, in that bushel. But that's not what our children were meant for. They were meant to be a light in this dark, dark world. They were meant to shine in a community.

Embracing A Church Community for Your Family

I heard recently that 80

I think the reason I find that statistic so heartbreaking is because that means that every church is missing a huge portion of the body of Christ. And they are missing the opportunity to be the body of Christ to special needs individuals.

Taking a special-needs child to church is hard. We've moved three times in five years, so I know what it is like to walk into a new church, wondering if it will be a good fit for your family, and if they will be accepting of your children.

Of the ten or so churches we have attended in the last five years (until we found a church we wanted to call ours after each move), only two were not a good fit for our children.

But the other churches we went to? They were welcoming. Sure, it took a little extra work getting to church and making sure the church workers knew about our children's needs. Sure, I'd spend a little extra time in the room with my boys, making sure they were settled and safe before I left to join the church service. But to have an hour or an hour of a half each week to focus on my own walk with God, to sit and worship with my husband and not have to worry about my children, was glorious.

Parenting a child with special needs means we'll always be advocating for them, even in a church. There are times I've had to set up a meeting with the children's ministry pastor to express our concerns or needs for our children, and they've always been accommodating, eager to help and love on my children.

A church is the community that will help you bring your child to Jesus, just like the friends did for the paralyzed man in *Mark 2:4-6*. Jesus was teaching in a home and there were so many people gathered that no one else could get in.

> Some men came, bringing to him a paralytic, carried by four of them. Since they could not get him to Jesus because of the crowd, they made an opening in the roof above Jesus, and after digging through it, lowered the mat the paralyzed man was lying on. When Jesus saw their faith, he said to the paralytic "Son, your sins are forgiven."

That is the church community you need for your child. A community that seeks to bring your child into the presence of Jesus, though it requires extra effort to do so. A community that will sacrificially love your child for an hour a week, just as you do the remainder of the week. We're not meant to bring our children to Jesus alone.

No church is perfect, but I promise you, there are churches out there with people ready and willing to love and teach your child. And there is a church community out there that will encourage you in the challenging journey of embracing this special life. We're not meant to go this journey alone. As it says throughout Scripture, we are meant to be in fellowship with a church family.

"Let us not give up meeting together, as some are in the habit of doing, but let us encourage one another" *Hebrews 10:25*.

You may have been wounded by a church before. I myself was badly hurt by something a preschool church worker said about my son. In that case, you need to begin the process of forgiving the individuals in the church who hurt you. I didn't want to return to that church because of that one individual's hurtful words, but I realized I had to forgive the woman for her words and her not understanding my son. The church is composed of fallen, sinful people who can hurt us intentionally or unintentionally. We are called to forgive those who hurt us.

You may feel the church you are attending (or attended in the past) isn't very accommodating of your child's needs. I encourage you to set up a meeting with the church's pastors and share with them your concerns and your child's needs. More often than not, they are more than willing to accommodate for your children and your family's needs. They have no way of offering you the support you need if they do not know what kind of support you need.

Or you may feel a calling to help your church establish its own special needs ministry. Talk to your church's pastors about it, seek a few other special needs parents or church members willing to help you, and help mold your church into a welcoming community for your child and other special needs children.

You may be not attending a church at all. I encourage you to pray about where God would have you fellowship with other believers. There are churches with amazing special needs ministries to help support your entire family. There are churches that don't have a special needs ministry, but they have supportive pastors and church members ready to include your child and your family. There are churches with great small groups/Bible studies to offer you and your husband the community and growth you desperately need.

Your child's needs may be too great to take them to church on Sundays. I have two special needs mama friends whose children both have significant medical needs, and so they have banded together with their husbands, creating their own family-friendly church service at one of their houses. I had the opportunity to join them once and it was a beautiful time of fellowship for everyone. I encourage you to pray about ways you can get involved with a group of believers. Maybe it is attending a church's Bible study, or inviting a few friends into your home for weekly Bible study and fellowship. Or you and your husband getting involved in a nearby church's special needs ministry support group. My husband and I have always found that spiritual growth seems to happen most in small groups, where you can learn and be vulnerable with a group of people you get to experience life with.

Pray about how God wants you and your family to be involved with an encouraging church family and what role He would have you play in that church. It is in a nurturing community of believers that we have the most opportunity for spiritual growth and to experience the joys of being part of the body of Christ.

Reflection Questions

1. Who are the people in your life you can sit and share life circumstances with? Who would you like to connect with?
2. What blessings have you experienced by having support and friendships during this special needs journey?
3. What can you do to let your children shine in your community?
4. What has been your family's experience with attending church?
5. What steps do you need to take to get more involved in a church community that is supportive to your family?

Chapter 11

Releasing Worry

I saw a meme once that said a worried mother can do better research than the FBI. And I have to admit, I think it's true. We become mamas on a mission, determined to do all we can to help our children succeed and worrying about any area where they are struggling.

I mentioned in a previous chapter that a special needs parent experiences similar stress level to that of a combat soldier. As special needs mamas, there are more things we must do for our children than parents of neurotypical children. More appointments, more medical terms in our vocabulary, more questions about the future. Those who have children with medical issues, seizures, food allergies, or impulsively run into dangerous situations must always be on alert, just like a combat soldier. We worry about things mothers of neurotypical kids can't even imagine worrying about. We have less free time and oftentimes little or no support. It makes sense that we would be stressed and worried. But, both God and Jesus commanded us to not worry. To trust Him.

Oh, if only it were that easy!

Releasing Anxiety

If your child was standing in the middle of the street and a car was coming, your body would release a lot of the stress hormones cortisol and adrenaline, which would compel you to action and enable you to run faster or lift things you never could have before the adrenaline rush. You would be able to rescue your child before he or she would be injured. Afterward, your body would feel jittery because of that release of adrenaline and your heart would be pounding for quite a while, even after your child was safe and sound in your arms on the side of the road. It is a fight or flight response that we were designed with to keep us alive if we or someone we love is in danger.

But, today, millions of people constantly feel like they are in this fight and flight phase. The cortisol keeps pumping. The heart-pounding worries never cease. This is the nervous disorder of anxiety, which can be accompanied by compulsive behaviors, intrusive thoughts, panic attacks, insomnia, and other health issues. This is not the worry and anxiety we'll be talking about in this chapter.

If you experience worry from time to time (like I do currently)

then the next section will be right up your alley. But if you experience chronic anxiety, you will need help to overcome it. I
struggled with this kind of anxiety for about three years after my
younger son was born, around the same time my older son was
diagnosed with several disorders. I spoke with my doctor who
prescribed me medication, and I also went to a Christian counselor to help me process my grief and anxiety. I shared my anxiety with my husband, a few family members, and the ladies in
my Bible study who prayed for me and offered me the support I
so desperately needed. Do not hesitate to get help if you need it.
This is a medical issue that cannot be dealt with on your own and
cannot simply be prayed away, as powerful as prayer is.

Although God can bring peace to your heart and mind and has
the power to heal, a medication to regulate those stress hormones is oftentimes exactly what we need. Do not feel like you
are a bad Christian for needing to be on medication. We don't
make diabetics feel like if they would just pray harder they would
be healed and not need insulin. And yet that is something those
struggling with mental health issues experience—that if you just
prayed harder you'd be better. We should not feel bad for taking medication for depression or anxiety until our hormones are
regulated.

What Jesus Says About Worry

Now, back to our conversation about worry. Worry doesn't help
us get anywhere, but it sure can stop us from being productive

and trusting God. The word worry is derived from a word that means to "strangle or choke."

Jesus told a parable about a sower spreading seed in *Mark 4*. The sower represents God, and the seed is the word of God, His promises and truths. There was a group of people who never really received the word. There were others who heard the word, but didn't really rely on the word and they died. There are others who "hear the word, accept it, and produce a crop–thirty, sixty, or even a hundred times what was sown," (*Mark 4:20*). But the seed we're interested in is the third type of seed, those who "like seed sown among thorns, hear the word; but the worries of this life, the deceitfulness of wealth and the desires for other things come in and choke the word, making it unfruitful" (*Mark 4:18-19*).

Oh, how often I find myself that third type of seed. I love God, I raise my hands in praise to Him and surrender on Sundays and during Bible studies, but when I come across a circumstance that seems overwhelming, well then, cue the thorns. Especially when it comes to my sons.

Worry can keep us trapped, stuck, paralyzed, and unable to do anything productive.

There's a passage in *Matthew 6:25-34* that's probably familiar to you. It's the "do not worry" passage, about how we're not supposed to worry about what food we'll eat or what clothes we'll wear. But one time I read through it and realized it said "do not worry" three separate times. In biblical times, the number three meant completion. Jesus' ministry was three years long and He prayed three times in the garden before His death. He hung for three hours on the cross. He laid in the tomb for three days. All to symbolize God's completion of His plan. So when Jesus says something to the people not once, not twice, but three times, He's expecting them to pay attention and get that this is an important message, a command.

I want you to fill in the blanks below and make this passage applicable to your own life and circumstances. Put your own top three worries in the blanks.

"Therefore, I tell you (your name) _____, do not worry about (circumstance) _____, (circumstance) _____, or about (circumstance) _____. Look at the birds of the air, they do not sow or reap or store away in barns, and yet your heavenly Father feeds them. Are you (and your child/ren) not much more valuable than they? Can you by worrying add a single hour to your (or their) life?"

And then to top it all off, just in case people didn't think He was serious about this command to not worry, Jesus calls a person who is worrying "of little faith." He says this again to His disciples when they feared they'd drown in the storm (*Matthew 8:26*).

Ouch. I personally don't want our Lord and Savior to call me a woman of little faith. But sometimes it's really hard to not worry. To not trust. To try to control things on our own. And so we must become intentional with our thoughts and worries, so as soon as we realize we're worrying, we can turn our worries over to God.

What Paul Says About Worry

Paul wrote a letter to the Philippians telling them to "Rejoice in the Lord always. Again, I say, rejoice" (*Philippians 4:4*). If Paul had to say it twice, it must be important and something we need to be reminded of often because it's challenging to do. But if we are rejoicing in the Lord, we are focused on the good things, the blessings in our lives, rather than our challenging circumstances. Like Peter, who was able to walk on water until he took his eyes off of Jesus and became fearful of the wind and waves and began to sink, so we too must be focused on God, His blessings, and His will for our lives.

The next verse, *Philippians 4:5*, says "Let your gentleness be evident to all. The Lord is near." I've found that when we get anxious and fearful, we get irritable and demanding. The disciples were terrified they would drown in the storm and demanded that He care about the situation. But Jesus was near the entire time. And He was disappointed they didn't trust that He would help them through the storm. When we are fearful and anxious, that is all the more reason to seek God, and we are likely to find His peace and comfort and protection then.

Paul then continues, "Do not be anxious about anything, but in everything, by prayer and petition, with thanksgiving, present your requests to God" (*Philippians 4:6*).

This is not just an encouragement to not be anxious. We are commanded to not be anxious because we have God on our side. He is there for us. He doesn't want us to be fearful and anxious. He wants us to trust Him. Just like we encourage our kids not to worry, that everything will be ok, that there will be a reward after something hard they have to go through, etc. We want our kids to turn to us when they are afraid, and we want to offer them comfort and reassurance.

And finally, we are told to present our worries and requests to God "with thanksgiving" (*Philippians 4:6*). I used to overlook the praying with thanksgiving part. I mean, I understand why we are to be thankful for all our blessings, and to thank God for them. But I didn't understand why we should be thankful when we are presenting our concerns to Him. He hasn't answered it yet, so there's nothing to be thankful for, right?

Wrong. There's a lot to be thankful for when praying your concerns. For example, as I mentioned previously, for a while I was really worried about whether I should homeschool my older son. I felt I needed an answer sooner rather than later. I researched online, I journaled about it, I talked to my husband and other homeschooling moms about it. But I wanted God to just give me an answer. And then, I read this passage in Philippians, and I decided to submit this worry to God and pray with thanksgiving. And I prayed something like this,

God, I really am worried about this homeschooling thing. I don't know what to do. But I'm glad you do. I'm glad you're in control. I'm glad you're right here with me and will be beside me no matter what we do. I'm thankful I live in a country where my child can receive an education and where I have the freedom to educate my child myself. Help me to know what you want for my son. And give me the strength to do whatever is best for my son. Thank you that You are my strength.

See all that thanksgiving there? It wasn't there before, but once it entered my prayers, I felt free. I felt the worries transferring from my helpless hands into the loving hands of our all-knowing Father. And though I didn't get an answer about homeschooling right away like I wanted, I felt a peace I hadn't in a long time and had an opportunity to enjoy my children more while I learned to trust God and His timing. And in doing so, God's answer became clear to me (and my husband!). It wasn't like a voice telling me what to do. Just a peace as I played with and taught my children that assured me I could indeed homeschool them. That He would give me strength. But that what my child needed was to grow in social skills and language. That my son was getting that from his preschool more than he was from me. And how much more would he get it in kindergarten? God has given us the peace to put our children in public school, and we are watching them thrive and flourish and bloom like never before. And should we feel like God is telling us to pull them out of public school and homeschool them, then we will. For now, we are simply submitting to God's plan and seeing the fruit of our obedience.

I encourage you to take something you're worried about and pray about those things with thanksgiving and honesty. You can write it out in a prayer journal or just pour out your heart before God. Take all the time you need.

Are you feeling any peace about the situation yet? I hope so, because this passage continues on to say that if we present our requests to God with thanksgiving, "the peace of God, which transcends all understanding, will guard your hearts and minds in Christ Jesus" (*Philippians 4:7*).

I love how it's worded in the Message version.

> Don't fret or worry. Instead of worrying, pray. Let petitions and praises shape your worries into prayers, letting God know your concerns. Before you know it, a sense of God's wholeness, everything coming together for good, will come and settle you down. It's wonderful what happens when Christ displaces worry at the center of your life.

Ah, beautiful, isn't it? I absolutely love the part about letting praise and thanksgiving "shape your worries into prayers."

Casting Our Worries

God knows we will worry. It is natural. But He has told us to cast our anxieties and worries on Him. In fact, we are commanded to cast our worries in both the Old and the New Testament.

Psalm 55:22 "Cast your cares on the LORD, and he will sustain you; he will never let you fall."

1 Peter 5:7 "Cast all your anxiety on him because he cares for you."

Casting is the act of letting something go, of complete surrender and leaving the results up to fate or to God. In *John 21*, the disciples were fishing and would cast their nets in hopes they'd catch some fish. They had been casting nets all night long and Jesus comes along and tells them to cast their net one more time on the other side of the boat, and they obeyed, hoping this time they'd catch something. And they caught so many fish they couldn't fit them all in the boat!

In *Matthew 13* the farmer cast seeds, hoping they would bear fruit. Some did, and some did not, falling among thorns, rocky soil, or eaten by the birds. But the farmer cast them anyway, out of obedience to his calling, in hopes that something would grow and yield a crop.

Similarly, we must cast our worries on God, surrendering them them into His hands, letting go of our attempts to control the situation, and let God work and do something beautiful with our offering our worries into His loving hands.

How do you cast your anxieties and worries to God? The secret is actually contained in the verse before what we just read. "Humble yourselves, therefore, under God's mighty hand, that he may lift you up in due time" (*1 Peter 5:6*).

To be humble means to think of yourself as less important than someone else. It means to view God as bigger than your own will, desires, and plans. To relinquish control of your life and that of your children and to trust Him. To recognize when we're not trusting Him and releasing our worry, just as we did earlier in this chapter. And praying with thanksgiving, because we know our God is faithful.

Don't feel guilty about worrying. Instead, focus on becoming a woman of faith. A woman who turns to prayer when she feels worried. God is molding us into warrior women of faith. You are a great mom and daughter of God. He is pleased with you and He loves you and wants to provide for you. And He wants you to walk like you believe it.

Reflection Questions

1. Do you have general worries, or are you struggling with chronic anxiety? If you are struggling with anxiety, what steps should you take to get the support you need?
2. Are you more like the seed sown among the thorns choked by the worries of the world or like the seed sown on good soil?
3. How often do you find yourself praying about your worries and turning to God when you are anxious?
4. What things are you most worried about? How can you pray with thanksgiving regarding each worry?
5. How can praying in humility help lessen your worry?

Chapter 12

Embracing Your Children

One day I went for a walk through a neighborhood. I saw a lone flower growing between a crack in the sidewalk and a brick rock wall. At first I felt sorry for this flower. There was a beautiful garden just five feet away from this flower boasting a kaleidoscopic display of color. Surely that was where the flower belonged. Yet, here was this flower, all by itself, growing in a place I couldn't imagine would be beneficial for anything to grow.

But then my perspective changed. And I was proud of this flower. It did exactly what it was created to do: spread its roots, grow, bloom, and share its color and beauty with the world, despite its unusual circumstances. It could have withered up and died, but it was flourishing.

And it got me thinking about my own children. They are not in the garden I expected them to grow in. There's a part of me that so desperately wants to scoop them up and put them in the garden with the other flowers. A part of me that fears that strangers will pluck that flower because it doesn't seem to belong there.

But I want to embrace the unique way they are blooming: their own rate of development, their personalities, their abilities, their passions, and yes, even their quirks.

And when I focus on them that way, I see they are indeed blooming, showing off their unique colors to this world desperate for a little color and joy in it.

And that makes me one proud and blessed mama.

Embracing Their Progress

It's so easy to see how far our children have to go to catch up with their peers. To see their weaknesses and their struggles. But we have to be intentional to focus on the positive. To focus on each and every victory, no matter how small it may seem.

In the Genesis account of God creating the world, notice He said "It was good" after everything He created. He didn't just say "It was good" when it was all done. We must do that too. Celebrate the little victories as well as the big.

Throughout Scripture there were ways people honored what God had done. They built altars. Named their children after God's characteristics or actions. Collected memorial stones (*Joshua 4*).

Around the time my older son was three, I started a blog for our family and closest friends about the boys' monthly progress reports, recording new words and skills gained. Sometimes I would post videos of their latest words or skills. And every year I would post a longer video of me talking with my kids so I could see how much improvement my children made in their speech. And whenever I felt discouraged that they weren't making much progress, I'd go back to the blog, look at where they were at a year ago, and then two years ago, three years ago, and remember how far they have come. Remember how hard we worked to get where we are now.

I needed that visual reminder of the progress they made because it can feel overwhelming to see how far they have to go. It was my way of helping me gain perspective and focus on the victories and not the struggles.

Philippians 4:8 says, "Whatever is true, whatever is noble, whatever is right, whatever is pure, whatever is lovely, whatever is admirable–if anything is excellent or praiseworthy–think about such things."

I had to be intentional to focus on the positive about my childrens' development. I learned to celebrate every milestone and every single inch in between, instead of just focusing on the next milestone and feeling there was never a light at the end of the tunnel. When you see how far your child has come, you realize you've made quite a bit of progress, and that will give you the encouragement to keep moving forward.

Embracing Their Hearts

As a mom, it's in our very nature to compare. We compare ourselves to other moms, and our children to other children.

In some ways comparison can actually be a good thing. For example, if I hadn't compared my older son to his peers, I wouldn't have noticed there was such a significant delay in his gross motor skills and got him the help he needed from a physical therapist at such a young age. I could have easily listened to the pediatrician who said not to worry, that all babies develop at their own pace, especially boys, but I saw the delay and I insisted on getting him help.

But comparison can become a problem if we allow it to make us feel like we or our children are not doing enough, or if we or our children are better than others. Like Theodore Roosevelt said, "Comparison is the thief of joy." Feelings of either failure or superiority are the result of comparison rather than living as the original masterpiece God created you, me, and our children to be.

In 1 Samuel 16, God tells Samuel that He knew Saul wasn't the best king for them, but He gave the people what they wanted. They wanted a king who was tall and handsome and strong, and Saul was that. But he didn't have a heart after God or a heart for the people of God. So God sent Samuel to the house of Jesse where one of his sons would be named king.

Samuel saw Jesse's oldest son, Eliab. Like Saul, he was tall and handsome. Samuel was sure Eliab would be the appointed one.

> But the Lord said to Samuel, 'Do not consider his appearance or his height, for I have rejected him. The Lord does not look at the things man looks at. Man looks at the outward appearance, but the Lord looks at the heart' (1 Samuel 16:7).

God showed me I was looking at my sons' developmental milestones and how they might appear to others, more than I was looking at their precious hearts. God delights in our children and in their hearts more than we will ever know this side of eternity. When I started focusing on my children's hearts rather than just their development, I got a glimpse of the little men God created them to be.

For example, with my older son I worried constantly about how far developmentally he was behind his peers and so I worked diligently to try to catch him up to his peers. But all I felt was a constant feeling of failure and I wasn't able to enjoy just being with my son when all I could think of was the areas we needed to work on. By learning to embrace his heart, I began to truly enjoy and appreciate the child that he was and the joy that he brought to everyone around him. I began to fixate less on his development and his weaknesses and truly see my sweet, smart boy who has a great love for babies and science and engineering. Doing so gave me the opportunity to plan activities that would nurture those strengths and passions he had and I was able to watch him blossom, doing activities that made him excited and come alive.

With my younger son, I found myself preoccupied with his anxiety and meltdowns and impulsive nature. Once I started to look past those overwhelming behaviors, I saw what his little heart was aching for. He wanted a little more attention from his stressed-out mama. A little more structure in our days, since each day's schedule varied based on our appointments and errands. And once I started getting more intentional about giving him the structure and support he needed, I found his anxiety and meltdowns becoming less common, and his heart and emotions calming. I watched his heart bloom and become kind and sensitive to others around him once he felt secure.

To be honest, there are days I still have to remind myself to stop worrying so much about their outward appearance, their behaviors, their skills, and instead zero in on their precious hearts. But it's worth it, because focusing on their hearts gives me the opportunity to love and support my children the way they needed to be loved and supported, and I am watching them bloom in their own beautiful way.

Numerous verses in scripture tell us to guard and protect our hearts. Our hearts are very precious to God, and we are to care for, nurture, and protect our childrens' hearts as well. Whenever possible remind your children that their identity is not in their diagnosis and weaknesses, but their identity is that of a beloved child of God. Remind them of how God gifted them, remind them of their strengths when they are feeling discouraged by their struggles, and let them know how much they are loved by God and by you. Let them know that you are proud of them.

If you haven't already, determine which of the five love languages each of your children responds to the most, and be intentional to show them love in their own love language. Showing your child love in a way that speaks directly to their heart will plant seeds of love, security and confidence in your children so they can bloom.

Embracing Their Passions

It's easy to see our child's weaknesses, and figure out how to help them in those areas of weakness. We take them to therapies and help with homework and do all we can to help them compensate for their weakness. But our children have strengths that need to be nurtured too.

Kristine Barnett wrote a fascinating memoir called *The Spark: A Mother's Story of Nurturing, Genius, and Autism*[7]. She decided to focus not on her non-verbal son's multiple areas of weaknesses with his severe autism diagnosis, but instead focus on what he was interested in, which was space. She took him to see the stars at night, to the planetarium, to lectures on astronomy, and she watched her son come alive. He became more interested in the things of the world when he was fed what interested him. He began to talk. And before long he was studying physics and astronomy on his own, taking college classes at age eleven. He still couldn't tie his own shoelaces or understand how to interact appropriately with everyone, but he could write mathematical equations I will never be able to understand.

Think about how you feel alive when you get an opportunity to do something you love. Wouldn't that also be true for our children?

It's a concept that greatly challenged and encouraged me in my parenting.

I encourage you to write down your childrens' interests and passions. Plan activities to make sure they get to experience those things and grow those passions. And watch their excitement as they get to experience something that makes their little hearts feel alive.

For us, it's going to the beach yearly. Every trip to the beach, the kiddos learn new words, gain new skills, and are beaming from ear to ear.

My younger son loves farm animals. I remember taking him to the farm and a petting zoo one time, watching his face light up every time he saw an animal he recognized, and saying the sound the animal makes. By the end of that trip he had gained five new words.

My older son loves building things and Legos. So one year for his birthday we took him to Legoland Discovery Center in Atlanta. That kid was in Lego heaven. He was watching what other kids were doing and imitating them. He was asking to go on his favorite ride again. He was fully alive.

When you nurture your child's hearts and their passions, when you focus on their strengths and how far they've come, you'll find so much joy in who God created your child to be. You'll see just how fearfully and wonderfully they are made (*Psalm 139:14*). And you'll proudly watch your child bloom, showing off their unique colors to the world.

Reflection Questions

1. In what ways do you focus more on your child's outward appearance rather than his/her heart?

2. What are the latest victories in your child's development? Is it easier for you to focus on the victories or on the struggles?

3. What can you do to show your children you embrace them for who they are?

4. What are your children excited and passionate about? What can you do to help nurture that passion?

5. Write a letter to each of your child(ren) telling them all the things you are proud of about them, all the things you know they are passionate about and gifted in. Keep this letter in a place where you will be able to read it again when you are feeling discouraged and need a reminder of another perspective. Consider giving a copy to your children when they are old enough and need some encouragement.

A Letter from the Author

Dear Friend,

I'm so glad you joined me on this journey of embracing this special life! There's a few things I wanted to share with you.

First of all, I want to share how much I believe God meant for you personally to have the messages embedded in this book.

There were times I could not write anything in this book for months at a time, because I was going through some struggles of my own. Yet another diagnosis for one of my boys. Another move to another state. Another bout of depression or anxiety or health issues. Such is our special needs journey, right?

Or I would get into negative thinking mode. Thinking that I was not qualified to write this book, that no one would read it, or worse, that no one would like it.

Fear and insecurity were constant companions in this book-writing process. The fear was so crippling, that if it was up to me, I wouldn't have finished, let alone published this book. I'm a woman of comfort, rather than courage. But just as God told me to embrace so many things in this life, He also told me (repeatedly) I had to embrace writing this book. To be obedient regardless of my fears or feelings. To write and share and be vulnerable even when I didn't want to.

And after enough nudging, I would find myself back in the pages, writing down the thoughts and lessons and messages God kept teaching me or I kept learning along this journey. And then when the book was done, I procrastinated on publishing it. The fear was overwhelming—what if no one read it, or liked it? Did I really want people knowing all these struggles I had in my heart? And then God whispered the all-familiar word "release" to me, reminding me I had embraced the message of this book, but now it was time to release it out into the world, to the hands of those who need this message.

I prayed that this book would find its way into the hands of the women who needed this message. You, reading this book, are an answer to my prayer.

Finally, I want to leave you with a bit of encouragement. Above my desk is a picture of a mother and baby giraffe. And it says simply "I didn't become the mother I thought I would be. I became the mother my child needed."

You, my friend, are a great mother. The exact mother your child needs. Keep being you, the you God created you to be, and the people around you will be blessed as you continue to embrace all this special life holds.

Keep loving God, your husband, yourself, your children, and the people around you to the best of your ability. Keep letting go of those things God does not want you to hold on to and keep embracing all the good things He has for you.

By doing so, you will find yourself flourishing despite the challenges of our special needs parenting journey.

I pray we will flourish in faith and embrace this one beautiful, special life we have been given.

Love,

Jenn

Scriptures To Pray for Your Child(ren)

A few years ago, after reading Beth Moore's amazing *Praying God's Word*, and Stormie Omartian's *The Power of a Praying Parent*, I discovered the joy of praying Scripture for my children.

I looked up Scriptures that related to the areas I was already praying for my children and wrote them on a list in my prayer notebook. There are fifteen I pray the most, and I compiled them here for you. Insert your child's name into each Bible verse, make it personal to their situation, and you'll find power and joy in praying Scripture for your child.

1. Pray for your child's *salvation*. Just because your child may be delayed does not mean we haven't been commanded to teach our child about Jesus and salvation and shouldn't long for our children to be saved. "But because of his great love for us, God, who is rich in mercy, made us alive with Christ even when we were dead in

transgressions—it is by grace you have been saved" (*Ephesians 2:3-5*).

2. Pray that your child would *love others*. Lots of our children struggle with social skills. Pray that your child would continually grow in their social skills and learn how to make friends and how to love others. "Love is patient and kind. It does not envy, it does not boast, it is not proud. It is not rude, it is not self-seeking, it is not easily angered, it keeps no record of wrong. Love does not delight in evil but rejoices with the truth. It always protects, always trusts, always hopes, always perseveres" (*1 Corinthians 13:4-7*).

3. Pray for your child's *growth*. They may be delayed in several areas, but pray that he or she would always "grow in wisdom and stature and in favor with God and with man" (*Luke 2:52*).

4. Pray for your child's *speech*. Your child may be nonverbal, have delayed speech and language, or have no issues with speech whatsoever. Pray that each of their words (spoken and unspoken means of communication) would be a sweet apple of gold that others could treasure. "A word fitly spoken is like apples of gold in settings of silver" (*Proverbs 25:11*). (Daily I would pray for new words, and praise God for each new "sweet apple of gold" they learned. This became one of my favorite Scriptures for praying for my boys.)

5. Pray for your child's *future*. It may be scary, wondering what their future will hold, but daily entrust their future to God. "'For I know the plans I have for you,' declares the

Lord, 'Plans to prosper you and not to harm you, plans to give you hope and a future'" (*Jeremiah 29:11*).

6. Pray for your child to grow in *wisdom*. Pray that their mind would focus and they would grow in the areas they struggle. Pray they would continue to flourish in their areas of strength. Pray also for you, their teachers, and their therapists—that all who teach your child would have wisdom to know how to teach your child. "For the Lord gives wisdom, from his mouth come knowledge and understanding" (*Proverbs 2:6*).

7. Pray that your child would experience *health*. Lift up any medical concerns you have regarding your child. Pray also for wisdom for their doctors and specialists to know how to help your child and wisdom for you regarding how to care for your child's health. "I pray that you may enjoy good health and that all may go well with you, even as your soul is getting along well" (*3 John 1:2*).

8. Pray for your child to *love God*. We not only want our child to believe in God, but to love Him and long to follow Him in their lives. "You shall love the LORD your God with all your heart and all your mind and all your strength" (*Luke 10:27*).

9. Pray for your child's *perseverance*. Our children have to work extra hard to learn to do things that come naturally to so many others. Pray that they continue in strength to learn and grow and that they would "...never tire of doing what is good" (*2 Thessalonians 3:13*).

10. Pray for your child's *protection*. Whether medically frag-
ile, a wanderer, impulsive, or just like any human being
who could get hurt or sick, we must cover our children in
prayer for their protection, and trust that they are safe in
God's hands. "He will cover you with his feathers, and under his wings you will find refuge; his faithfulness will be
your shield and rampart" (*Psalm 91:4*).

11. Pray your child would have *peace* in their heart. So many
of our children struggle with anxiety. Pray that they would
have peace from all their anxieties and have peaceful sleep.
"Peace I leave with you, my peace I give to you. I do not
give as the world gives. Do not let your hearts be troubled
and do not be afraid" (*John 14:27*).

12. Pray for your child's *purpose*. Pray that your child would
be used for God's glory. Pray that your eyes would be
opened to what God is doing in your child's life. Pray that
your child would grow into the man/woman God has created them to be. "For we are God's masterpiece, created
in Christ Jesus to do good works, which God prepared in
advance for us to do" (*Ephesians 2:10*).

13. Pray that your child would grow in *self-control*. Whether
impulsive, defiant, sensory-seeking or calm, cool and collected, pray that your child would learn to "... live self-
controlled, upright and godly lives ..." (*Titus 2:11-12*).

14. Pray that your child would grow in *obedience*. The more
our children learn to obey their parents, teachers, and therapists, the safer they are and more likely they are to thrive
in all environments, current and future. "Children, obey

your parents, for this is right. Honor your father and mother, the first commandment with a promise, so that it may go well with you and that you may enjoy long life on earth" (*Ephesians 6:1-3*).

15. Pray for your child's *courage*. There are so many new, challenging things for our children to accomplish each day. Pray that they would have boldness to try new things and overcome any unhealthy fears they may have. "Be strong and courageous. Do not be afraid, do not be discouraged, for the LORD your God will be with you wherever you go" (*Joshua 1:9*).

Acknowledgements

They say it takes a village to raise a child, but I've learned it takes a tribe to write and publish a book, and I am forever grateful to every person in my tribe.

First and foremost, I would be lost without God in my life, and this book would not exist without His sustaining grace, the lessons He taught me while traveling on this special needs journey, and the continual nudgings to write them into this book. I've long dreamed of writing and publishing a book, and God in His goodness gave me everything I needed to write this one.

A huge thank you to my husband for partnering with me in life and in the creation of this book. I am so blessed to have you in my life, you are an awesome provider, husband, father, and friend. Thank you for being someone I could brainstorm with and who provided me the means and the support to write this book. Thank you for offering your amazing tech and design skills to format the book and design the cover–you helped me execute my dream and make this book a reality.

To my editor Sandra Peoples, thank you for blessing me with your editing expertise and encouraging comments.

A huge shout out to the amazing ladies who know the struggles of special needs parenting and took the time to read my book and offer honest feedback: Sarah Broady, Sara L. Foust, Melanie Gomez, and Maegan Keel. Your partnership will always be appreciated and cherished.

To family and friends who encouraged me along this writing process, without your enthusiasm for this book it would still be a document on my computer.

And finally, to you my readers, thank you for reading and joining me in this journey of embracing this special life. I pray this book blesses you while reading it as much as it blessed me to write it.

About the Author

Jenn Soehnlin is the mother of two boys who both have special needs and who are both precious blessings. When she's not busy taking her lads to yet another appointment, she can be found snuggling with her boys (hubby included), curled up with a good book, enjoying a  walk through nature, or at a coffee shop writing and blogging at http://www.embracing.life.

References

[1]: Lysa TerKeurst, The Best Yes: Making Wise Decisions in the Midst of Endless Demands (Nashville: Nelson, 2014)

[2]: Beth Moore, David: Seeking a Heart Like His (Nashville: Lifeway Christian Resources, 2010)

[3]: Linda Dillow, Calm My Anxious Heart: A Woman's Guide to Finding Contentment (USA: NavPress, 2007)

[4]: Stormie Omartian, The Power of a Praying Parent (Oregon: Harvest House Publishers, 1982)

[5]: Ridiculous. Dr. Caroline Leaf. Church Media Group, Inc via http://drleaf.com/media/page1/ TedX

[6]: Renee Swope, A Confident Heart: How to Stop Doubting Yourself and Live in the Security of God's Promises (Michigan: Revell Books, 2001)

[7]: Kristine Barnett, The Spark: A Mother's Story of Nurturing, Genius, and Autism (New York: Random House Publishing, 2013)

42035917R00092

Made in the USA
Lexington, KY
12 June 2019